GOOD & NOBLE HEART

"If I will change,
everything will change
for me."

Jim Rhon

GOOD & NOBLE HEART

300 Days Through The Bible
To Reveal Your Identity And Purpose

JOHN BRADBURY

ISBN: 9781727276459

Connect on Instagram, Facebook, and the web **@johnbradbury.co**

Introduction

GOOD & NOBLE HEART is more than a book; it's a journey.

It's my path out of insecurity into a life of impact, and I believe it's yours as well.

After two decades of wanting to make a difference but struggling to understand how, **this book changed my life.**

For three hundred days in a row, I listened to four chapters of the Bible, then wrote a short devotional focused on what I felt God revealed to me about my identity.

I was amazed day after day as the Holy Spirit highlighted the secrets of living a fruitful life.

As the year progressed, I became increasingly convinced of one thing-- **to glorify God with my life and bear much fruit, I have to change the way I think.**

The title, GOOD & NOBLE HEART, comes from the parable of the sower in Luke 8:15,

But the ones that fell on the good ground are those who, having heard the word with a noble and good heart, keep it and bear fruit with patience.

God showed me that the only variable in that story is the soil, or the condition of our hearts.

The Father is constant, Jesus is faithful, and His Word remains the same, **so the fruit of our lives depends on how we think about ourselves.**

If we receive the ideas He gives us with a good and noble heart, we will produce fruit that adds value to our lives, others, and the world.

So, as you journey through this book, my prayer for you is simple, yet profound.

I pray that you learn to think about yourself the same way God thinks of you.

If you get that, you get everything.

Blessing to you and your family,

John Bradbury

DAY 1: GENESIS 1 - 4

Shame & Blame

Then the LORD God called to Adam and said to him, "Where are you?" So he said, "I heard Your voice in the garden, and I was afraid because I was naked; and I hid myself."

God designed you in His image and likeness-- you are creative, speak things into existence, and have dominion on the earth. Your body is designed to fellowship with the spirit realm, encountering God and receiving from Him on a daily basis. **Your normal state is communion with the Creator.**

God created you to live CONFIDENT and PURE, never thinking through the lens of shame. Your nature is to be awesome, to be the kind of person who looks for challenges and enjoys responsibility.

You are a SON or DAUGHTER of the living God. SATAN'S LIES ARE ALWAYS INTENDED TO UNDERMINE YOUR IDENTITY.

He wants you to THINK like an ORPHAN. If you believe his lies, it will manifest two ways: shame or blame. Shame is not normal for the believer. Instead, we should live with extreme confidence in the finished work of the cross. If you feel shame, it means one of two things; either you don't believe what Jesus did for you worked, or you blame someone else for your actions.

Blame says, "My life is not my responsibility. I don't control my thoughts or choices, and when I do wrong, instead of REPENTING, I shift the responsibility to someone else. Nothing screams that you are listening to your enemy like blame.

Jesus changed all of that. He says that if you take responsibility for your life, CHANGE THE WAY YOU THINK, and believe in Him, He will restore you as a SON or DAUGHTER of God.

Intimacy without shame, fellowship with the Creator, and dominion on the earth are yours as a child of God.

DAY 2: GENESIS 5 - 8

The Thoughts Of His Heart

Then the LORD saw that the wickedness of man was great in the earth, and that every intent of the thoughts of his heart was only evil continually. But Noah found grace in the eyes of the LORD.

It's a sad story, the story of Noah. It's a story of redemption and covenant, of restoration and bravery; but the loss of life was enormous.

How did it come to that? Genesis 6:5 tells us. Speaking about the general state of humanity, it says, "that every intent of the thoughts of his heart was only evil continually."

The way people thought of themselves was: "I'm the kind of person who doesn't care about the Creator, takes whatever I want, feels like an orphan, won't take responsibility, and blames others for my actions."

That kind of thinking led to a world full of chaos and violence. The whole story screams, "WE NEED A SAVOIR!" **But Noah found grace in the eyes of the LORD.**

Grace is the desire and power to do the right thing and please God. It is what creates the environment that keeps you righteous. So how did Noah do it? **The thoughts of his heart were different than everyone else's.**

He considered himself the kind of person who walks with the Creator just like his great-grandfather Enoch. He was in the line of Seth, the fulfillment of the promise to Eve. His father named him Noah because he was going to fix the curse on the ground.

And he called his name Noah, saying, "This one will comfort us concerning our work and the toil of our hands, because of the ground which the LORD has cursed." Genesis 5:29

He thought of himself as a friend of God, as someone destined to change the world, and he found grace in the eyes of the Lord.

DAY 3: GENESIS 9 - 12

I Will Make You Great

Now the LORD had said to Abram: "Get out of your country, From your family And from your father's house, To a land that I will show you. I will make you a great nation; I will bless you And make your name great; And you shall be a blessing.

The covenant that we continue to receive blessings from, God's covenant with Abraham, is all about IDENTITY.

God said to Abraham, "I will make your name great," and he said yes. God was looking for someone to **say yes to being great** so He could bless all of the families of the earth.

You know where I'm going with this, don't you? **God is still looking for people LIKE YOU who will be GREAT so He can use you to add value to the planet.**

The future state of the world is not dependent on a decision God will make; He already decided to bless ALL THE FAMILIES OF THE EARTH. He initiated the covenant with Abraham that led to Jesus that led to you.

YOUR WILLINGNESS TO BE GREAT IS THE DECIDING FACTOR WHICH WILL DETERMINE THE FUTURE STATE OF THE WORLD.

I know it's uncomfortable-- it's easy to shrink back and stay in our comfort zones.

But that was yesterday.

Your willingness to keep growing as a person, improve your skills, increase your confidence, fellowship with the Holy Spirit, understand the Scriptures, love people, seek spiritual gifts, and think of yourself as a leader is critical to the next generation's future.

Are you willing to be great?

DAY 4: GENESIS 13 - 16

And He Believed God

Then He brought him outside and said, "Look now toward heaven, and count the stars if you are able to number them." And He said to him, "So shall your descendants be." And he believed in the LORD, and He accounted it to him for righteousness.

Abram had everything-- the wife he desired, wealth, a relationship with God, favor with people-- except the one thing he wanted. He longed for a son he could leave a legacy to.

Perhaps that's where you find yourself. You try your best to be grateful, and you are. You put real effort into staying content, but the longing won't go away. You love God, and you love people too. You are doing everything you know to do.

When you fellowship with God, He says stuff like, "Do not be afraid, Abram. I am your shield, your exceedingly great reward." AWWWW! I know you are, but I still want a child! Are you tired of prophecies, promises, and encouragement? Does your heart cry, **"How about a little fulfillment here?"**

Abram felt like that. God took him outside, made him one more promise, and then showed him the stars and said, "Look now toward heaven, and count the stars if you are able to number them. So shall your descendants be."

And Abram believed God.

What changed? Abram realized that the desire of his heart was not opposed to God's will for his life, but was put there by God to drive him to fulfill it.

EVERYTHING CHANGES WHEN YOU REALIZE THAT YOUR DEEPEST DESIRE WAS PUT THERE BY GOD AS A SIGN OF THE PURPOSE HE HAS FOR YOUR LIFE.

DAY 5: GENESIS 17 - 20

Why Did You Laugh?

And the LORD said to Abraham, "Why did Sarah laugh, saying, 'Shall I surely bear a child, since I am old?'

Why do we laugh when God speaks something over our lives that is the fulfillment of our heart's desires?

First, we laugh because we're hiding. God wanted to talk to Sarah, look her in the eyes, and prophesy into her the strength and courage to fulfill the word, but she was hiding. So instead, God spoke about her to Abraham. When we overhear the promise spoken about us, we often miss the grace that comes with it.

Second, we laugh because it's too painful to hope. Sarah wanted a child her whole life. After decades of dreaming and scheming, she lowered her expectations-- then God wanted to talk about it. Why bring this up when I finally settled on my fate? If what you are hearing from God isn't uncomfortable, you are probably ignoring some of what He is saying.

Third, we laugh because of timing. Sarah was old. After years of traveling and chasing a promise God gave Abraham, she wasn't jumping at opportunities anymore. Then word comes-- SOON. If you refuse to SLOWLY prepare your heart, skills, and relationship with God, and then QUICKLY pursue the promise when it's time, you will miss what God has for you.

Fourth, we laugh because of weakness. Sarah was beautiful, wealthy, confident, and loved by her husband. Sarah had many strengths, but God wanted to use her in her weakness. Why does God do that? We often bury our strengths and desires under layers of protection to guard against disappointment. Be ready for the word of God to stretch and challenge you.

Finally, we laugh because we don't understand the process. You are not the fruit, plant, or seed-- YOU ARE THE SOIL. Your job is to prepare yourself to receive the word from God, to nurture a good and noble heart.

DAY 6: GENESIS 21 - 24

The Control Dilemma

And Abraham said, "My son, God will provide for Himself the lamb for a burnt offering."

So here's the dilemma. You spend tons of time and energy becoming the kind of person to whom God can give a promise that will change the world. You fight through all the junk in your heart, believe God, and get the fulfillment.

With the fulfillment comes a sense of ownership and responsibility, and you want to be a good steward of the promise.

But then a situation arises where you have to choose between what you are sure is the sensible thing to do, and what you think God is saying. God says to make Hagar and her son leave and provide for themselves or sacrifice your son on an altar.

"But I don't want to! It's not wisdom. They're my responsibility. If I do that, I will lose control of the situation." EXACTLY.

CONTROL KILLS FRUITFULNESS.

The supernatural provision of God is on the other side of letting go and doing what God says. **The problem is that you're not SURE.** It's difficult because you don't know what will happen after you give up control.

GOD ONLY PROVIDES FOR HIS PLANS, NOT YOURS.

He makes the well of water and the ram for the sacrifice appear just in time, and He doesn't bother to tell you about it. That is why He is God, and you're not.

So do your job, and let Him do His. Nurture a tender, trusting, confident, humble, and believing heart. He controls the seed, weather, and fruit. You control the condition of your heart.

DAY 7: GENESIS 25 - 28

Urgency vs. Inheritance

And Esau said, "Look, I am about to die; so what is this birthright to me?"

The Bible says God HATED Esau because he valued his belly over his inheritance.

Ouch. Esau was in the line of Adam, Seth, Noah, and Abraham. His role was to bless all the families of the earth and lead to the coming of thc Messiah.

He stood to inherit land as far as the eye could see, abundant water, huge herds, and fertile fields. In other words, he was about to be INCREDIBLY RICH.

The Bible says this about Esau's father, Isaac: "The man began to prosper, and continued prospering until he became very prosperous; for he had possessions of flocks and possessions of herds and a great number of servants."

Esau grew up in an environment of incredible abundance, promises, and favor. In that context, Esau said, **"Look, I am about to die; so what is this birthright to me?"**

HOW OFTEN DO WE DO THE SAME THING?

We are supposed to disciple nations and leave an inheritance to our children's children. We should live in heavenly places with authority over all the power of the enemy. **We are the solution to every problem on earth.**

But so often we miss what God wants to do in and through our lives because we never learn to manage our emotions.

Let's tend to our hearts in such a way that BIG IDEAS from God grow, bear fruit, and change the world. Don't allow the urgency of your emotions choke out the purpose God has for your life.

DAY 8: GENESIS 29 - 32

The Big Transition

So Jacob was greatly afraid and distressed.

Everyone starts out serving someone else's vision or trying to meet others people's expectations. But deep inside, you know there's MORE.

Jacob listened to his mom, fell in love, and connived his way to a measure of success, but it wasn't enough. He knew there was more, but he was scared to death to pursue it.

He tried all the usual CHRISTIAN SUPERSTITION tactics he could think of to get God to help him, but God had something else in mind-- an IDENTITY UPGRADE.

Jacob needed to KNOW that he wasn't the same old guy and face his greatest fear, "what if I don't have what it takes?" So God set up a wrestling match.

Have you ever been there, wrestling with God about your future?

It's not enough anymore to manipulate your way through life; you need to KNOW that you are a PRINCE WITH GOD.

When God changed Jacob's name to Israel, He changed his IDENTITY from deceiver to prince with God. In the process, Jacob won his wrestling match with fear.

To BE WHO YOU WERE BORN TO BE, YOU MUST FACE YOUR GREATEST FEARS.

DAY 9: GENESIS 33 - 36

Doubt vs. Destiny

"Your name is Jacob; your name shall not be called Jacob anymore, but Israel shall be your name."

There is something deep inside you that longs to be significant, experience real love, feel beautiful, have more than enough, solve big problems, make someone proud, and leave a legacy.

God made you in His image-- He wants you to be like Jesus. Jesus came to earth and endured the cross, not out of duty, but because He deeply desired you. He knew what He wanted and went after it with passion, and God wants you to live the same way.

Why are we so scared of our desires? We love to quote verses that say our hearts are evil, and we pile layers of protection over our hopes to guard our hearts against disappointment.

Jacob came out of the womb fighting to be first. He wanted to be a Prince With God, but his parents named him Deceiver. He lived with something to prove, but like most of us, kept sabotaging himself.

Then God said, "You are a Prince With God," affirming his life-long desire. But DOUBT began to bully him, saying, "Who do you think you are?" If you're not careful, after God calls you a Prince With God, doubt will keep you thinking like a deceiver.

Hear the Father saying to you, "You're a Prince with God. Your not Jacob anymore, so why are you still running scared? You're supposed to be living in the house of God, walking around like you own the place, thinking like you are friends with the Almighty."

DAY 10: GENESIS 37 - 40

Jealousy

But when his brothers saw that their father loved him more than all his brothers, they hated him and could not speak peaceably to him.

Joseph had it all. He was the best looking, the most intelligent, and a natural leader. But he was young and arrogant, and he didn't know how to use his favor to add value to others. His brothers were jealous, and longing for their approval, Joseph piled it on until they couldn't stand him.

Why does God load someone up with all of the good stuff, even while they are immature? We know from later in the story what God had in mind, that Joseph would save the region from famine.

But what if you're not Joseph in the story? What if God has highly favored some young punk to save your life, but right now it all seems unfair? God gives some people five talents, expects them to double it, and then takes from the little guy and gives it to the one with ten. Then He makes them your boss, and doesn't wait until they are mature and loving to do it.

The problem is that while you are irritated with them, God is planning on using them to bless you, and He doesn't tell you ahead of time. He expects you to use humility and discernment to recognize the favor on them, submit, and help them succeed.

God develops leaders with incredible favor on their life to bless a group of people. Those who recognize that favor while they are still immature and help them, get swept along in the stream of blessing, and those who don't miss out. Be slow to judge the gifted but immature leader-- **if you can only be led by perfect people, you may find yourself hungry during the famine.**

DAY 11: GENESIS 41 - 44

Every Idea Needs An Identity

"Can we find such a one as this, a man in whom is the Spirit of God?"

"I HAVE A DREAM," Martin Luther King said, but if all he had were a dream, nothing would have come of it.

God planted that dream in the heart of a confident and compassionate identity that was willing to learn, lead, speak, and not give up.

Pharaoh had a dream as well. He had the most important idea of his generation, the plan that would save the entire region.

The idea was great, but what happens next?

If your heart is unprepared to grow the idea God gives you it gets wasted, and then the game begins. I call it Christian superstition.

"O God, you said... , why isn't it happening? Please, tell me again, just one more confirmation. Don't you like me anymore? How long is this going to take?"

If Joseph doesn't use Pharaoh's dream to make an action plan and skillfully execute it for the next fourteen years, everyone starves to death.

Can we please stop the Christian superstition game?

Yes, God likes you, and you heard from Him.

But will you prepare your heart with the confidence, humility, resilience, gratefulness, peace, and GRIT you need to do something with the idea?

DAY 12: GENESIS 45 - 48

Leading People Out Of Shame

"But now, do not therefore be grieved or angry with yourselves because you sold me here; for God sent me before you to preserve life."

When Joseph encountered his brothers years after they sold him into slavery, he knew there was a wall between them.

For him to have a voice in their lives, he had to break down that wall.

Whether they knew it or not, they had a huge pile of shame and guilt built up in their hearts, which manifested as fear because of Joseph's position of influence.

For Joseph's brothers to trust him, they needed that shame and guilt removed.

Now Joseph had already forgiven them, but that was not enough. Forgiveness sets the forgiver free, but another step is needed for the offender to be influenced by the forgiver.

Joseph gave them a way to forgive themselves by showing them the bigger story and the way God turned the situation around for good.

He took the initiative to identify the area of shame they were struggling with and give them a way out.

For people to listen to or follow you, they must do it willingly. If they feel manipulated in any way, it's only a matter of time until they get out.

It is the leader's responsibility to identify the shame that others live with and show them the bigger picture so that they can get free.

Until someone can forgive themselves, they can't move on.

DAY 13: GENESIS 49 - Exodus 2

Embracing Uncertainty

Then he said, "Who made you a prince and a judge over us?"

Some things are certain: God loves you, you belong with Him, Jesus is the only way to the Father, and the increase of His government and peace will never end.

However, your future fruitfulness is not guaranteed.

Moses found this out the hard way. He thought because he survived at birth, was raised in the palace, and wanted to help his people that they would embrace him as their deliverer, but the exact opposite occurred.

After a 40 year lesson in humility and an encounter with God, Moses eventually delivered his people. But late in life, he missed out on the promise land because of the same problem; he presumed the results were inevitable.

Most of us go to great lengths to avoid uncertainty. We try to control everything down to the smallest detail, and we attempt to paint God in a corner so that He has to bless us. **But life does not work that way.**

People who do great things never get rid of fear, they learn to embrace it. They know that to succeed they are required to show up every day with excellence.

God will keep loving you, talking to you, and leading you. You can rely on Him 100%. But whether you embrace His words with a good and noble heart and bear 30, 60 or 100 fold is determined by the way you think about yourself.

Success is not guaranteed-- it is dependent on your thoughts, actions, and habits. Unless you cultivate your heart, God's Word will not bear fruit in your life.

DAY 14: Exodus 3 - 6

Who Am I?

*Moses said to God, "**Who am I** that I should go to Pharaoh, and that I should bring the children of Israel out of Egypt?"*

Our first excuse is always, "Who am I?"

But when you are talking to the God who calls himself, "I AM," it seems like a pretty lame excuse.

He says, "ANYTHING IS POSSIBLE AT ANY TIME, ANYWHERE BECAUSE I AM."

God is so confident in His identity and made you in His image, "Who am I?" just isn't going to stop Him.

He always calls us before we know who we are because He loves talking us into becoming who He created us to be.

EXTREME CONFIDENCE is one of God's most defining characteristics, and when He comes and lives inside you, He expects you to feel the same way.

He is not waiting until you're perfect to call you to do great things, He is starting right now.

When you understand the revelation of the extreme power that lives inside you, extreme confidence will be the natural response.

DAY 15: Exodus 7 - 10

Control At Your Own Risk

Thus says the LORD God of the Hebrews: "Let My people go, that they may serve Me."

There is one guaranteed way to experience God's anger: use your influence to manipulate others for your benefit.

Jesus is very adamant about this, and He does not play favorites. No one is safe if they cross this line, even those whom He set up as leaders.

Now don't get me wrong, Jesus loves leadership. He chooses people like Moses to speak up, make decisions, gather, influence, and set His people free from their bondage.

There is no better way for people to develop than in a group of loving relationships led by an empowering leader. God designed it that way.

However, if you use your influence to do anything besides lovingly equip and develop people, look out!

Pharaoh learned this the hard way. God decided to make an example out of him so people would still be talking about it thousands of years later.

So, listen up parents, employers, teachers, ministers, managers, government officials, and leaders-- the fear of the Lord is real.

Stay under His authority and follow His agenda to empower people and you will experience His blessing, but start using people for your agenda and watch out!

The book of Exodus is like a big sign hanging in every generation saying,

"CONTROL AT YOUR OWN RISK!"

DAY 16: Exodus 11 - 14

Defining Moments

"So it shall be, when your son asks you in time to come, saying, 'What is this?' that you shall say to him, 'By strength of hand the LORD brought us out of Egypt, out of the house of bondage.'"

I love encounters with God. I love feeling His presence, hearing His voice and saying "WOW" when He comes through just in time with exactly what I need.

But let's be honest, significant encounters don't happen very often-- that's why it's essential we make the most of them.

God wanted Israel to remember the story of their deliverance from Egypt for generations to come so He told them to hold a yearly feast and to set apart all the firstborn of the animals and children to the Lord. He wanted them to turn the one time encounter into repeatable habits that would reinforce the message. So how do we do it? How do we take a significant moment in time and turn it into habits?

Here are a few things I've learned:

- Take advantage of the power of the moment. The emotion will eventually wear off, so use it while it's there to learn everything you can. Follow up quickly and go deep into research about what you learned while the grace is still there.
- Write it down! You don't think you will forget, but you will.
- Talk about it with some trusted people. Your brain can only process so much coming in; sharing what you learn allows you to acquire the rest.
- Pay attention to the implications. Ask the questions, "What does this say about God?" and "What does this say about how God thinks about me?"
- Create new habits based on the implications of the encounter. Ask, "If this is true, what should I do about it?"
- Refuse to be discouraged by the struggle. There is no failure, only winning and learning.

DAY 17: Exodus 15 - 18

Every Seed Is A Soil Test

But some of them left part of it until morning, and it bred worms and stank.

"What is it?" the Israelites asked when God answered their prayers.

We all do the same thing, don't we? We ask for something, and when God answers our prayer, we don't recognize it.

If you pray for a hot meal, then wake up to a layer of little seeds on the ground, you would say, "What is it?" too.

So often we ask for health, and God answers with a coach. We pray for money, and He tells us to give something away. We ask for revival, and He leads us to pray. We ask for a breakthrough, and we wake up with a new idea.

Most answers to our prayers come as SEEDS with conditions attached to them.

The children of Israel learned this lesson, albeit grudgingly. God gave them fresh Manna every morning, but there was a certain way to collect and eat it..

Why? **Because every seed is a soil test.**

If you can follow instructions, submit to authority, get up early, remember what you learned, use everything you received, and prepare ahead of time, then you will get the benefit of the Manna. If not, then you miss out.

God knows that His words have POWER, He is never just talking.

Depending on the state of your heart, every word He says will either judge or empower you. So every time He speaks (or answers your prayers), He is trying to draw you into BECOMING the kind of person who can steward what He says.

DAY 18: Exodus 19 - 22

What Are The Implications?

"You shall be a special treasure to Me above all people; for all the earth is Mine. And you shall be to Me a kingdom of priests and a holy nation."

I have a friend who is a physical therapist, and he is very good at his job. He invests in ongoing education, is mentored by the best in the business, studies best practices, treats hundreds of patients, and gets excellent results.

Recently we were together in a prayer meeting, and the Lord spoke to him prophetically: "God wants you to be wealthy." Based on my experience and discernment, as well as the witness of others, I am confident that this word was from God. I felt the excitement of the Holy Spirit when I heard it.

In a situation like this, the question to ask is, **"If this word is true, what are the implications?"** Here are some that I thought of:

- God gets excited about the prosperity of His children.
- Because my friend's prosperity correlates to his practice, God must have hundreds of people who are living with pain that He wants to heal.
- God desires to establish several new relationships that foster prosperity and health in our community.
- God has creative ideas to share with him in the future.
- God wants to increase his influence.
- God cares about the desires of his wife and kids and wants to use him to bless them.
- God trusts him and wants to increase that trust through a deeper relationship.
- Because he is a giver with a heart to fund the ministry, God has some big plans for the future that need funding.

I'm sure there are more, but you get the idea. When God speaks to us, it is not just encouragement. **His word releases power to change our future if we believe it.** What has God spoken over your life? Consider the implications and align your heart with His purpose for your life.

DAY 19: Exodus 23 - 26

Seated In Heavenly Places

And there was under His feet as it were a paved work of sapphire stone, and it was like the very heavens in its clarity.

In Exodus 24 we read these words: "so they saw God, and they ate and drank."

Are you serious? A bunch of guys eating lunch with God and there is only one line about it?

I think I would have been a little more descriptive-- what an incredible experience that must have been.

There you are, on a pavement of sapphire stones as far as the eye can see. Can you imagine it?

They ate lunch standing on an endless blue ocean with God himself.

Did you know that amazing event in history is now the current reality for every believer?

You are seated with Him in heavenly places right now because the Holy Spirit dwells inside of you.

Your ability to walk worthy of the Lord, please Him, and be fruitful depends on your ability to access that vast expanse of knowledge in heaven.

The Spirit of God who is in heaven is also in you, and He searches that endless supply of knowledge and shares with you the relevant data as you need it.

All you have to do is pay attention.

DAY 20: Exodus 27 - 30

Tending His Presence

Aaron and his sons shall tend it from evening until morning before the LORD.

No longer is it necessary to offer a sacrifice for sin because Jesus became the sacrifice once and for all. No longer is it necessary to consecrate a High Priest because He is the High Priest forever.

You are the temple of the Lord and together with all the saints are being built into a dwelling place for Him on the earth. You have the privilege of tending to His presence that lives inside you.

His glory will continue to increase in the earth-- that's inevitable. But the question is, will it increase IN YOUR LIFE?

So how do we tend to His presence?

We pay attention to His voice.

We remain grateful.

We offer a sacrifice of praise.

We keep a whole heart.

We speak kindly to ourselves.

We are generous with others.

We regularly gather with others for worship.

We quickly obey.

We listen to those who are bearing fruit.

DAY 21: Exodus 31 - 34

Don't Take No For An Answer

Moses took his tent and pitched it outside the camp, far from the camp, and called it the tabernacle of meeting.

The people of Israel were a mess. While Moses was meeting with God on the mountain, they were down below making a golden calf to worship.

God told Moses, "those are your people" and Moses was like, "no way, those are your people." Then God said, "I can't go with you into your promise because you're too stubborn. If I come to your camp, I'll consume you."

Moses pleaded with God, but He wouldn't budge. Then Moses got a brilliant idea. He thought, "if you can't come into the camp with us, I'll move my tent outside the camp, and we'll meet there."

So he took his tent and moved it way outside the camp and called it the tabernacle of meeting, and God loved it! God met with Moses whenever he wanted and talked to him face to face.

Moses refused to go without the presence of God, so he found a workaround. He saw the glory of God, lead the people with the wisdom of God, and experience friendship with God. Moses was also able to identify all the hungry ones in the camp. He refused to take "no" for an answer; he would not leave God's presence behind to pursue a promise.

Perhaps you are in a similar situation. Are your family, friends or coworkers a mess? Maybe your church doesn't value the presence of God.

Then take your "tent" and go outside the camp. You control your thoughts, choices, attitude, and actions. Take the time you have control of and invest it in the presence of God. Refuse to move on without getting to know His ways and seeing His glory, and pretty soon you will start attracting hungry people into your life.

DAY 22: Exodus 35 - 38

One Willing Step

Then everyone came whose heart was stirred, and everyone whose spirit was willing.

God deserves your whole heart, but it's not always easy to give. Our fears, selfishness, past mistakes, shame, grief, bad examples, and stubbornness impede our progress towards thankfulness from a pure heart.

So what does God do? He meets you wherever you are and invites you to take one willing step forward.

Remember when Moses was on the mountain meeting with God and the people were down below making a golden calf to worship? Their disloyalty broke God's heart, but He did not give up on them.

He saw that the people enjoyed taking the beautiful things and making stuff, so He invited them to use what they had to worship Him instead of a worthless golden calf.

God will meet you wherever you are and invite you to take one willing step.

Do you like to talk? Great, use your mouth to glorify Him.

Do you like to make stuff? Excellent, willingly use your creativity to worship Him.

Do you enjoy work? Good, use your diligence to seek first His kingdom.

Do you like to write? Use your craft to empower others to love Him.

Do you enjoy serving? Willingly care for those on God's heart.

ONE WILLING STEP TOWARDS WORSHIP TODAY ATTRACTS THE ANOINTING INTO YOUR LIFE AND STARTS YOU ON THE PATH TO WHOLENESS.

DAY 23: Exodus 39 - Leviticus 2

Living Aware Of His Presence

And the glory of the LORD filled the tabernacle.

Jesus is the greater Moses.

As Moses led God's people out of slavery into the promised land, Jesus leads us out of bondage and into the Kingdom of God.

As Moses built a dwelling place for God on the earth, Jesus is building you into a resting place for His presence.

You are the temple of God, but not all believers reap the benefits-- **only those who live aware of His presence get results.**

LIVING AWARE OF WHAT JESUS DID FOR YOU, YOUR NEW IDENTITY, AND THE PRESENCE OF GOD RESTING ON YOUR LIFE IS THE ONLY WAY TO EXPERIENCE FREEDOM.

Only those who practice daily worship feel clean and act clean.

Only those who daily seek to hear and obey His voice feel like they are leading a meaningful life and make a difference.

Only those who take care of their body and soul feel confident and energized.

Only those who daily receive a fresh word from God in prayer feel motivated and do great things.

Only those who practice being AWARE of His presence feel close to God and live lives worthy of Him.

DAY 24: Leviticus 3 - 6

Living Aware Of Your Sin

When he realizes it, then he shall be guilty.

Do you know what the biggest problem of living under the law was-- constant awareness of sin. Feeling guilt and shame was normal, and it sucked the life out of you.

Jesus changed that forever.

Guilt is the awareness that I did something wrong, and shame is the awareness that there is something wrong with me. Neither one has a place in the life of the believer.

So why do most of us still live with the crushing feeling that we are always messing up?

We feel like screw-ups because of what we think about all day long. Awareness is everything.

Jesus forgave you, adopted you, and gave you access to the Holy Spirit. That access changes your life, but only if you are aware of it.

Believers in Jesus can still sin, but it is not in their nature anymore. Sin is the exception, not the rule. When we sin the Holy Spirit convicts us, we humble ourselves, repent, make things right, and God forgives us. The sense of guilt goes away, and we live completely unaware of it.

The same is true for shame. Our hearts are good and noble, and we should live feeling like they are.

JESUS RESTORED CONTROL OF YOUR MIND BACK TO YOU, SO YOU CAN CHOOSE TO THINK ABOUT WHATEVER YOU WANT. SET YOUR MIND ON THE THINGS OF THE SPIRIT, AND YOU WILL BEGIN TO REINFORCE THE TRUTH OF THE GOSPEL IN YOUR LIFE.

DAY 25: Leviticus 7 - 10

Those Who Come Near

"By those who come near Me I must be regarded as holy; And before all the people I must be glorified."

"You don't work for me; I work for you." That's what I have been saying to the Lord lately. It comes from Galatians 2:20 where Paul says, "I have been crucified with Christ; it is no longer I who live, but Christ lives in me; and the life which I now live in the flesh I live by faith in the Son of God, who loved me and gave Himself for me."

God can put one drop of anointing on a person or give them an idea and make it blow up. He has access to the heart and mind of every person on the planet and can with one decision promote someone beyond what you can imagine, but **He is impossible to manipulate.**

If you are going to be someone who comes near and knows God, you must live by a different standard. I'm not talking about getting your sin forgiven, being adopted, and going to heaven. To get those things you humble yourself and repent, believe in Jesus and follow Him.

I'm referring to those who want to come near. If you're going to carry the same anointing that Jesus, walk in His power, and get similar results you will be required to SUBMIT, OBEY, LOVE, and HONOR the Father at the same level that Jesus does.

THERE IS NO SUCH THING AS WALKING IN THE ANOINTING AND HAVING YOUR OWN AGENDA. JESUS DOES NOT WORK FOR YOU; YOU WORK FOR HIM.

If you are called to come near and carry the anointing, prepare for a marathon, not a sprint. It's a lifelong relationship with the Holy Spirit built on TRUST-- you trusting Him, Him trusting you, and you trusting yourself.

This is my lifelong quest, to earn His trust and know Him. How about you?

DAY 26: Leviticus 11 - 14

Holy And Whole

You shall therefore be holy, for I am holy.

The cloud of His Glory rests over the tabernacle, and the Manna appears on the ground every day.

The Creator is talking face to face with Moses, and what does He want to talk about? Eating right and avoiding disease.

Huh?

The same God who parted the Red Sea, appeared in a fire on the mountain, rained down food every day for 40 years, and performed all the plagues in Egypt is talking face to face about what to eat. **Interesting.**

God cares about your body, health, relationships, finances, and work. While He is healing you instantly, He is talking to you about eating healthy and exercising. He is the God of the book of Acts and the book of Proverbs.

To God it is all the same thing; there is no natural and supernatural to Him. He does not divide secular and sacred, human and spirit, visible and invisible. Everything is visible to His eyes.

He wants you to walk in both, understand both, and stop dividing the two.

Jesus came to empower you, which means you are no longer a victim in any area of your life.

You are a SON or DAUGHTER of the Creator with DOMINION in both the natural and spiritual realm.

IF YOU ARE A SON OF GOD, EVERYTHING IS NATURAL. WHAT LOOKS SUPER TO OTHERS IS NORMAL FOR YOU.

DAY 27: Leviticus 15 - 18

Make It Worse

You shall afflict your souls.

Jesus came preaching, "the way you are thinking isn't working, so change it." A big part of the thinking change was recognizing that He was the Savior and that the Kingdom was near. But I think there is more to it, a principle that is easy to miss. I call it the **make it worse principle.**

God used it with the people of Israel when He instituted the Day of Atonement. Once a year they were to evaluate themselves while the High Priest went into the tabernacle to make atonement for their sins.

But Jesus taught it in the Sermon on the Mount in Matthew 5, applying the principle on a broader scale. It goes something like this. Every area of your life should be blessed or fruitful, and the way to become fruitful is first to make it worse. We should set aside to accurately and objectively evaluate the RESULTS we are getting in our life. Here is Jesus' checklist in Matthew 5:

- What areas am I week in spiritually? If I can admit my poverty in those areas honestly, then I attract His grace to help build me up.
- What deep losses have I experienced? If I genuinely mourn the losses I have suffered, then He will heal my heart.
- How have I mistreated others? If I choose to be gentle with others, He will be gentle with me.
- Where have I been apathetic? If I pursue with hunger right thinking, then He will fill me with revelation.
- Where have I been wronged? If I forgive those who have hurt me, then He will show me mercy.
- Is there sin in my life? If I repent, He will reveal more of Himself to me.
- Is there any conflict between me and someone else? If I initiate peace with them, then I will feel like a Son.
- Is there someone opposing me unfairly? If I accept that pursuing greatness will result in people misunderstanding me, then God will reward me openly.

DAY 28: Leviticus 19 - 22

Perfection vs. Greatness

No man of the descendants of Aaron the priest, who has a defect, shall come near to offer the offerings made by fire to the LORD.

The law demands perfection, and perfectionism is a very demanding taskmaster.

It requires everything but empowers nothing, leaving it's victim helpless and frustrated.

But Jesus is different.

He encourages the weak to come to Him because He has what the law never did, GRACE. Grace empowers greatness in us and gives more than it requires.

That's why Jesus could encounter a guy with thousands of demons who lived in a graveyard and welcome Him into His presence. **He always had more to give than He required from others.**

He did not keep His distance from lepers like the law commanded, choosing instead to cleanse them.

Jesus desires greatness from us, the same way a great coach demands greatness from his players.

Because of His commitment to empowering us and His unlimited supply of revelation and love, requiring greatness is the only reasonable thing to do.

PERFECTIONISM IS A CRUEL TASKMASTER, ALWAYS REQUIRING AND NEVER EMPOWERING.

GRACE ALWAYS EMPOWERS MORE THAN IT DEMANDS.

DAY 29: Leviticus 23 - 26

Commanded Blessing

Then I will command My blessing on you in the sixth year, and it will bring forth produce enough for three years.

God can say a command and make your work three times more profitable.

That's cool, but it's interesting that He doesn't do it all the time; He does it in response to intentional weakness.

- Don't plant anything one year, and I will make your harvest from the previous year multiply by three.
- Work six days and rest one day.
- Give 10% of your income away.
- Don't eat occasionally.
- Spend time talking and singing to an invisible God.
- Gather with others to worship.
- Forgive people who have wronged you.
- Don't plant anything once every seven years.

Why does God do stuff like that?

Honor. He enjoys you seeing the fruit of your labor most of the time, but He also knows that you need regular reminders of His power, and for that, you must choose weakness. By choosing to rest instead of work, give instead of keep, fast instead of eating, or pray instead of doing it yourself, you HONOR Him with your trust.

In that context, not when we are acting like victims, but when we CHOOSE to make ourselves weak, He COMMANDS HIS BLESSING on our lives and our fruitfulness increases.

EMBRACE THE RHYTHM OF REST. CHOOSE TO MAKE YOURSELF WEAK, AND HE WILL SHOW HIMSELF STRONG.

DAY 30: Leviticus 27 - Numbers 3

Preparing For The Promise

You and Aaron shall number them by their armies.

The path to your promise is littered with the dead dreams of those who thought that all they needed to get to fulfillment was a hope and a prayer.

When God calls you out of slavery and dangles the promised land in front of you, He is after more than just showing off His power.

The Christian life is not about being handed promises; it's about becoming a confident, emotionally whole, and focused person who can take what God gives them and grow it.

MIRACLES ARE THE NATURAL BY-PRODUCT OF SOMEONE WHO ORGANIZES THEIR LIFE AROUND HIS PRESENCE AND PROMISES.

God wanted the people of Israel to think of themselves differently. Sure, God was doing supernatural things in their midst, providing for them and speaking to them, but He was also organizing them, setting up leaders and preparing them for the next chapter of their lives.

His desire was for them to organize their entire lives around His presence in pursuit of His promise, willing to fight for what He said they could have. They were supposed to care about the details, think differently, set up habits and systems aligned with the promise, appoint leaders and keep the presence of God at the center of their lives.

Are you hoping Santa Claus brings a present for you someday because you have been a good girl or boy? Or are you militantly organizing your whole life in pursuit of His promise?

Guess which one is going to possess the promised land?

DAY 31: Numbers 4 - 7

If You Want More

This is the law of the Nazirite who vows to the LORD the offering for his separation.

Go to church, give money, do your devotions, pay your bills, love your family, be nice. Those are all good, but sometimes following the rules is not enough.

If you're hungry for more, consider the law of the Nazirite.

Jesus fulfilled the law; it is no longer required to make you righteous before God. But this principle, the Nazirite vow, made it through to the New Covenant; we see Paul doing it in the book of Acts. It's voluntary, so it's not really a law, but a method to get more of God.

Hungry hearts need to express themselves, and the kingdom of God rewards the hungry.

When you want more, here are some things you can do:

- Set aside some time-- the amount is up to you.
- Give up something that you will miss, but that is not sinful.
- Focus only on productive activity.
- Add a physical expression that reminds you of your time of devotion, like letting your hair grow during your time of commitment.
- Give a generous offering of time or money that is above what you would typically give.

A great example of this is Daniel's decision only to eat vegetables and drink water.

The result is greater tenderness, sensitivity, revelation, understanding, motivation, and grace.

DAY 32: Numbers 8 - 11

Intense Cravings

Now the mixed multitude who were among them yielded to intense craving; so the children of Israel also wept again and said: "Who will give us meat to eat?

God had a beautiful vision for His people. He was bringing them back into the land He promised Abraham ready to bless their socks off.

He wanted every family to own land and run a business that flourished. He dreamed of them becoming an example to all the other nations.

But there was a process to go through. Israel needed to get to know Him, think differently about themselves, learn how to live healthy and whole, stop feeling like slaves, get organized, come together as a nation, and fight for their desires. So God designed a year of transition so they could become the kind of people that would flourish in their promised land.

Then the unthinkable happened. Some of the people, instead of imagining God's vision for their lives, began remembering the days of slavery and longing to go back.

It would be like you or me saying, "Oh, I wish I could go back and sit on the couch and eat pizza whenever I feel like it, I miss those days," forgetting that we were addicted to pornography, overweight, lonely, and miserable.

God's vision is for us to be set in families, prospering financially, thriving in our relationships, free of all addictions, gathering to worship, fulfilling our purpose, and making a difference in the world.

He expects us to dream about it and INTENSELY DESIRE it. So when we long for the good old days where we had the illusion of control, it hurts His heart. **Don't allow your desires to drift back to the time where you didn't have to think, change, grow and learn. Maybe it was more comfortable, but it was MISERABLE.**

DAY 33: Numbers 12 - 15

Grasshopper Thinking

There we saw the giants (the descendants of Anak came from the giants); and ***we were like grasshoppers in our own sight****, and so we were in their sight."*

"Give Me 12 leaders, and I'll change the world," God told Moses. So Moses got his 12 best guys and sent them on a mission. They spent 40 days spying out the land, and 10 of them came back saying,

"Christians shouldn't be ambitious. Let's just follow the rules, be nice, try to stay away from giants, and be safe."

STUPID GRASSHOPPER THINKING!

The price for that kind of thinking is way too high. When you convince everyone that obtaining promises is too costly, you sentence them to live the rest of their lives slowly dying in the wilderness.

The very next chapter tells the story of a guy getting stoned to death for gathering sticks! That's the price of grasshopper leadership. That guy and his accusers were supposed to be preparing for war, but without VISION people cast off restraint.

"We are all going to die in this wilderness anyway, so what's the use. What difference does it make if I go after my dreams?"

God said the same thing to Jesus that He said to Moses, "Give Me 12 leaders, and I'll change the world," and the disciples turned the world upside down.

Jesus told us to disciple nations and make earth like heaven. So why do we think like grasshoppers? **The price for grasshopper leadership is too high to pay. It creates a hopeless generation nitpicking each other about nonsense instead of preparing for their promises.**

DAY 34: Numbers 16 - 19

The Fruit Test

Behold, the rod of Aaron, of the house of Levi, had sprouted and put forth buds, had produced blossoms and yielded ripe almonds.

God desires to bless us through leaders, but how do we tell which ones to listen to? Simple. It's called the fruit test.

God doesn't want us to judge people based on age, gender, race, experience, family history or place of origin because all of those things do not qualify people before Him.

Nor does He want us to judge people by their roots. They may have come from a terrible background, had bad examples, or made mistakes, but God is a redeemer, so that's not relevant.

Exterior trappings are not reliable either. Talent and education do matter, but the person with most degrees doesn't always produce the best results.

There's only one question that matters.

Are they growing the kind of fruit that you want to produce?

When God wanted the people to listen to Aaron, He had them put Aaron's rod in the Tabernacle.

It produced buds, blooms and ripe fruit at the same time, while the other leader's rods produced nothing.

Be careful not to discount the buds and the blossoms in someone's life in favor of only ripe fruit. They may be young and not have ripe fruit in an area of their lives yet, but their buds and blooms indicate future fruit.

YOU SHALL KNOW THEM BY THEIR FRUIT.

DAY 35: Numbers 20 - 23

Sick With Dread

Moab was sick with dread because of the children of Israel.

Aaron stood on top of the mountain, stripped of his Priestly garments and ready to die. His people missed their opportunity to enter their promised inheritance because of fear, and now they were wandering around in circles.

They had complained again, saying they wanted to go back to Egypt, **and Aaron was done**. He and Moses were so mad that they disobeyed a direct order from the Lord.

So there he stood. He was never going to see the fulfillment of the promise. He was never coming down.

Not too far away stood the enemy king, and he was scared to death.

Now Israel was not that scary if you ask me. They ran in fear themselves not too long ago and continued to whine about everything.

But the enemy watched from a distance sick with dread. They tried to curse God's people, but the curse wouldn't work. God would not agree with anything negative about His people.

Israel was immature and messy, but the enemy saw them as powerful. Even while God corrected them, He only had good to say in the hearing of the enemy.

That story gives me hope. Ultimately, what makes us awesome is belonging to God.

The enemy is sick with dread at us even while we are still immature.

IT SURE IS NICE BEING GOD'S FAVORITE.

DAY 36: Numbers 24 - 27

Zealous For His God

So the plague was stopped among the children of Israel.

Sweat dripping off his face and flush with anger he sprinted through the camp, javelin in hand.

He weaved around tents and leaped over cooking fires at full speed with eyes blazing, but somehow calm.

It all happened so fast. The problem existed for days, but this was too much, and Phinehas snapped.

This strange combination of deep compassion and righteous indignation rose up inside of him, and he just ran.

Somewhere along the way, he picked up a javelin; he was going to stop the problem, whatever it took.

Pure ZEAL drove him. Like Jesus cleansing the temple with a whip, Phinehas overflowed with passion and could not let the problem go on any longer.

AND GOD LOVED IT.

We stare at divorce, obesity, disease, drug addiction, anxiety, prejudice, and poverty all day long and sometimes we get numb.

We get caught up in the daily grind, and we grow accustomed to the plague, forgetting that we have the answer-- forgetting that we are the answer.

What is the plague you are called to stop?

Perhaps you should allow the zeal of the Lord to drive you to action and let Him tell you how along the way.

DAY 37: Numbers 28 - 31

Tested & Nurtured

Everything that can endure fire, you shall put through the fire, and it shall be clean; and it shall be purified with the water of purification. But all that cannot endure fire you shall put through water.

Yeah! You prayed, believed, worshiped, fought, endured, declared, gave, listened, obeyed, and you WON! Congratulations!

In the Kingdom of God, every breakthrough comes through the WORDS of God, and there are two kinds-- IDENTITY words and IDEA words.

When you win a spiritual battle, your reward is either an identity upgrade or an idea for the future. Both are awesome, but you don't get to use them right away. There is a process to go through before they are ready.

Identity words are about WHO YOU ARE. Idea words are about HOW YOU LIVE.

It is imperative to remember that your identity, or the way you think about yourself, must be tested. A great example of this is when God called Jesus His beloved Son, and then Jesus spent 40 days in the wilderness being tempted by the enemy.

But idea words are different. They do not need testing; they need nurturing. Like tender seeds cultivated by the farmer in good soil, idea words require care and attention.

When an idea is new, you can't expose it to the elements; you must handle it with care. You must keep remembering the word, watering it with prayer, thinking it through, talking about it, and caring for it.

REMEMBER, YOUR IDENTITY NEEDS TO BE TESTED, BUT YOU MUST NURTURE YOUR PROMISES.

DAY 38: Numbers 32 - 35

Fight For Each Other

We will not return to our homes until every one of the children of Israel has received his inheritance.

Every one of you are unique gifts that add value to the world. God dreamed of you long before you were born, thinking of the person you would be and the purpose you would have.

No one has the particular mix of identity, gifts, purpose, skills, desires, and ideas that you have, and God designed you to solve specific problems and bless certain people.

Your sphere of influence-- the people you care for, problems you solve, jobs you create, the creativity you add, the family you raise, products you produce, land you beautify, the business you grow and tribe you inspire-- is your inheritance from the Lord.

He wants you to own, love, grow, tend, and improve it. He created you to have dominion on the earth.

But that does not come without a fight. Enemies will try to keep you out of your inheritance. Lack of confidence in your identity, strong negative emotions, temptation and sin, persecution from others, and trauma in life all fight to keep you from taking your place.

So we fight. We refuse to lay down and let our enemies ruin our opportunity to make a difference in the world, but it's so hard to make progress alone.

But we are not in this alone. We may never fully realize our potential by ourselves, but if we fight for each other, anything is possible.

REFUSE TO QUIT UNTIL YOUR FRIENDS AND FAMILY HAVE COME INTO THEIR INHERITANCE.

DAY 39: Numbers 36 - Deuteronomy 3

You Must Not Fear Them

You must not fear them, for the LORD your God Himself fights for you.

Life is not an endless battle between our flesh and spirit; it is a fight WITH GOD against a common enemy to enter His REST and build something together.

Imagine a number line. Most of us start deep in the negative numbers, struggling to get back to zero, dealing with addiction, sin, insecurity, lack of confidence, unbelief, and fear.

Getting to zero means you feel, think, and act like a SON. You know who Jesus is and what He has done for you.

Once we feel like a SON or DAUGHTER, we start to work with God to develop people, solve problems, and bring the kingdom.

Where you are at on the line is not that important-- what matters is knowing that God is fighting for you, not against you. Remember:

- All you need is one victory to start making progress.
- Use the confidence of one victory to fight the next one.
- Fight with God, not against Him.
- When you get out of bondage, the process isn't over. Keep working with God to becoming more like Him your whole life.
- Success can be scarier than a failure if you let it. Remember, God wants you to succeed, so don't let fear stop you.
- Somewhere along the journey, you will transition from duty to desire. God is still leading you; He loves guiding us by our desires.
- You never graduate. You do not get less dependent on Jesus as you go, you get more.
- The farther along you go into the positive numbers, the bigger the problems you and God are tackling, and the more honor, respect, submission, dependence, intimacy, and partnership with Him is required.

DAY 40: Deuteronomy 4 - 7

The Big Story

For ask now concerning the days that are past, which were before you, since the day that God created man on the earth.

God created the planet with one thing in mind, a group of people made in His image which would voluntarily love Him. For that to be possible, people had to have glory, dominion, free will, and the ability to love.

Adam and Eve chose to embrace orphan thinking and willingly obeyed the voice of the enemy, giving Satan their dominion and creating a curse on the ground and the desire to control each other.

God began the restoration process with Seth, offering hope that He had a plan to fix the problem Adam and Eve created. Along came Noah, whom God used to reverse the curse on the ground. Then God called Abraham to act in faith, restoring our covenant with God.

Moses restored the understanding of right and wrong, and David reintroduced the idea of Godly leadership and prosperity. Then came the prophets, who restored the understanding of what was missing, a real relationship between God's people and Himself.

Finally, there is Jesus, God's only begotten Son, and the only human born without an orphan spirit. He proclaims the end of the restoration process and the beginning of the Kingdom of God. After a 40 year transition led by the Apostles, the age of Moses ended, and the Kingdom of God began.

So here we stand, with only one thing holding us back from bringing heaven to earth-- **revelation.** If we don't know the story and where we fit in it, we embrace poverty, ignorance, doubt, loneliness, powerlessness, and shame.

There is nothing left to do except to believe in Jesus, understand your place in the story, develop a confident identity, let God's words grow in your heart, learn how to access the power of the Spirit, and change the world.

DAY 41: Deuteronomy 8 - 11

Abundance

And you shall remember the LORD your God, for it is He who gives you power to get wealth, that He may establish His covenant which He swore to your fathers, as it is this day.

Abundance is a hard concept for most Christians.

It's defined as more than enough, but it may be better described by what it is not.

Abundance is the lack of loneliness, poverty, disease, boredom, scarcity, weakness, fear, and confusion, and it is God's desire for each of us.

Of course, there are times of testing in our lives to produce humility, confidence in who we are, and loyalty to God's word.

But tests are just tests; they don't define us.

We live by what God says, and nothing else, and His word over us is always, "YOU ARE MY BELOVED SON IN WHOM I AM WELL PLEASED."

So if circumstances, the enemy, other people, or my thoughts say otherwise, then they're wrong.

I live by, agree with, and fight using His words.

When I BELIEVE what God says about me, it unlocks supernatural abundance in and through my life.

His words enable me to add real value to others, think creatively, and generate wealth.

DAY 42: Deuteronomy 12 - 15

Uncommon

For you are a holy people to the LORD your God, and the LORD has chosen you to be a people for Himself, a special treasure above all the peoples who are on the face of the earth.

Every family is known for something. Yours is known for being so blessed that you run out of poor people sometimes.

You are a worshiper, a lover, who values His presence above all.

Every person in your tribe thrives in their unique inheritance.

You are special, like sunsets are special.

We are all priests and kings, every one of us. We believe God, love people, lead, care, give, and create.

You belong with us. Your nature is generous like the rain is generous.

You greatly desire and pursue dreams, just like your Father. It's in your nature to be awesome.

You don't tithe, give, forgive, bless, worship, love, and care because you have to-- you were born to. Mercy and goodness follow you around, and blessing overtakes you.

Your desires are good, your heart is good, your God is good, your nature is good, and your family is good.

You were born to win. You build, succeed, grow, prosper, give, and lend; that is the way your family has always done things.

IF YOU WERE BORN AGAIN, YOU WERE BORN AWESOME.

DAY 43: Deuteronomy 16 - 19

Staying In Rhythm

Remember the day in which you came out of the land of Egypt all the days of your life.

So here's the big question-- how do we EXPERIENCE more of what Jesus already provided for us? The answer: revelation, relationship, and remember.

When something is already yours legally, but you are not experiencing it yet, the problem is not you, the devil, or circumstances. The problem is the way you think.

Revelation is the key that opens every door in the Kingdom. The understanding of what God is like, who we are, and what is available to us opens up a whole new world of possibilities.

The more we understand Him and how He feels about us, the deeper we go in our relationship, through which God heals the broken places, empowers us with His Spirit, and begins to rub off on us.

The rhythm of it is beautiful, like a treasure hunt that always leads to more-- until we forget. **If revelation is our superpower, forgetting is our kryptonite**. We lose our power, confidence, peace, joy, and hope when we get distracted and lose sight of the truth.

So what is the solution? We build the rhythm of remembering into our lives so that we can't forget. We create habits that keep reminding us of our identity, God's glory, what He said, and the people He placed in our lives.

We listen to His word, worship, forgive, gather with others, receive communion, give, rest, share testimonies, write, pray, fast, preach, and read to remember what He has said and done.

Revelation is the key to growth, but remembering that revelation is the key to life. **Whoever has the best habits always wins in the end.**

DAY 44: Deuteronomy 20 - 23

The Softness Of Your Heart

For the LORD your God walks in the midst of your camp, to deliver you and give your enemies over to you.

Jesus said that Moses gave rules to the people because of the hardness of their hearts.

He could not change anyone's heart, only try to control their outward actions under threat of punishment and offer of reward.

No one felt clean, forgiven, adopted, safe, at peace. No one could rid themselves of the sense of guilt and shame; you just had to live with it and try to do the best you could.

You couldn't trust your desires. Everyone's heart was hard, and without external manipulation, nothing good was going to grow in it.

Sadly, much of the church still live like this.

But it does not have to be that way anymore!

Because of what Jesus did, your heart is great soil that grows everything God plants in it-- **if you change the way you think.**

Your heart is not a worn out piece of ground that requires harsh treatment; it's a luscious garden with fertile soil that quickly grows every seed that falls on its surface.

Your nature is to love. It's in your DNA to hear and obey His voice. No one has to manipulate you to do good-- you are good.

Nobility runs in your family. Confidence, peace, and joy are natural to you, like your heart pumping and lungs breathing.

DAY 45: Deuteronomy 24 - 27

Origin Story

So you shall rejoice in every good thing which the LORD your God has given to you and your house, you and the Levite and the stranger who is among you.

Many of us wander around aimlessly with no sense of identity.

We do not know our purpose, family history, or inheritance.

We don't want to be this way-- it's just the way it is.

The previous generation told us that the world is getting worse and that the church is a group of victims needing rescue.

They didn't worry about education, leaving an inheritance, or making the world a better place.

But things are changing.

God is calling fathers and mothers who are gathering us into families.

We are becoming the kind of people who know who we are, where we came from, and where we are going.

We receive our inheritance from those before us, make it better, and leave it for the next generation.

Our identities are clear, our purpose is grand, and our future is bright.

We embrace our history, family, gathering, ritual, and story, and we celebrate the increase that God has made possible.

DAY 46: Deuteronomy 28 - 31

By My Spirit

And the LORD said to Moses: "Behold, you will rest with your fathers; and this people will rise and play the harlot with the gods of the foreigners of the land, where they go to be among them, and they will forsake Me and break My covenant which I have made with them.

Israel witnessed the most spectacular miracles, but it wasn't enough. God spoke directly to them, but that wasn't enough. They had good leadership, but that wasn't enough. The law promised to bless obedience and curse disobedience, but that wasn't enough.

Supernatural provision, check. Angelic involvement, check. Specific instructions, check. The presence of God, check. Displays of power, check. But none of it was enough.

Perhaps it was just the hard-hearted people. Maybe, but when Jesus was on the earth He handpicked some guys and spent three years loving, teaching, and demonstrating the gospel to them, and one of them betrayed Him, and the others abandoned Him. Nothing seemed to work-- except one thing.

God told Zechariah, "Not by might nor by power, but by My Spirit."

Nothing from the outside can change us; only the ability, revelation, grace, and peace that comes from the indwelling of the Holy Spirit has ever produced a changed heart.

Those same guys who had experienced Jesus but still abandoned Him became radically different after the Holy Spirit filled them.

So why do we spend so much energy pursuing so many other things?

Wealth, health, wholeness, intimate relationships, peace, joy, love, and fulfillment comes from through the indwelling and fellowship of the Holy Spirit.

DAY 47: Deuteronomy 32 - Joshua 1

Time For Action

Now therefore, arise, go over this Jordan, you and all this people, to the land which I am giving to them.

Wow, it's been a long wait, or at least it feels like it.

So many promises, words, instructions, examples, and warnings, and now it's time to act!

It's time to come into your inheritance and start building your family, business, ministry, and legacy.

You are finally out of the negative numbers, and you are ready for some progress!

You've spent way too long wandering in circles where your actions did not seem to make any lasting impact.

If this is the season you are in, here are some things God told Joshua that you need to remember.

- Be strong and courageous. When you are doing something for the first time, you don't have enough experience to be confident, so you must act based on God's confidence in you.
- God will go with you, not do it for you.
- It's going to be a fight, but not a fair one.
- You must be obsessed with what God says. This is new territory, and all you have to go is what God tells you, so pay attention.
- Let your mouth lead the way. Until you have won your first fight, the most important thing is the way you talk.
- You gotta sell it. If you believe in what you're doing, invite others to come along.
- Just do it. To transition out of survival into your promises, you must change your mindset and take action.

DAY 48: Joshua 2 - 5

New Territory

When you see the ark of the covenant of the LORD your God, and the priests, the Levites, bearing it, then you shall set out from your place and go after it.

Does a new relationship, career path, baby, ministry, or business have you asking the question, "How do I know if I'm going the right direction?"

If so, make sure you start with the right assumptions: your heart is good, the Holy Spirit lives inside you, and God wants you to win.

Got it? Sweet, let's move on.

When Israel was heading into new territory, Joshua told them to follow the Ark, but to maintain some distance so they could adjust appropriately.

So how do we do that in our lives?

- Stay within the boundaries of LOVE.
- Stay within the principles of Scripture.
- Stay under authority.
- Be patient.
- Trust a few close friends.
- Don't let your emotions make your decisions.
- Ask the right questions.
- Do you feel at peace?

When entering new territory, follow the leading of the Lord, but keep a safe emotional distance so you can see clearly.

Cultivate a confident identity. Trust the Holy Spirit. Maintain peace.

Then when it's time act, go for it!

DAY 49: Joshua 6 - 9

Going Pro

So the LORD was with Joshua, and his fame spread throughout all the country.

Amateurs don't defeat Jericho.

Hobbyists don't change history.

Those who do things on the side never realize their potential.

Joshua was all in, fully committed to the task ahead. He showed up for work every day, put in his best effort, and trusted the results to the Lord.

Joshua was a professional. He was full time, rain or shine committed to what God called him to do.

Professionals show up every day for work. Professionals accept responsibility. Professionals pursue the mastery of their craft. Professionals win and lose, but they show up the next day anyway.

Amateurs have the same potential, but they do not reach it because they get stuck. Fear scolds them, procrastination stops them, and distraction robs them.

Professionals have the same feelings as amateurs, hear the same doubt whispering in their heads, and face the same obstacles-- **but they don't stop because they can't-- it's their job.**

Thinking of yourself as a pro is the only way to put in the kind of time, energy, and attention necessary to accomplish great things. Many of us have something great we want to do or be deep inside of us, but we keep putting it off because we have options.

UNLESS YOU HAVE TO, YOU WON'T.

DAY 50: Joshua 10 - 13

There's More To Do

Now Joshua was old, advanced in years. And the LORD said to him: "You are old, advanced in years, and there remains very much land yet to be possessed."

Our mandate is to make earth like heaven. What would the planet look like if we did our job?

I think it would be incredibly creative. Art, music, dance, architecture, writing, and cooking would go to new heights. It would be more diverse and unified at the same time. God loves making things different so that we can choose to cooperate.

Poverty would be nonexistent. Not only would everyone have meaningful work to do, but generosity would abound and create abundance. Peace would rule the day. War and violence would only exist in the history books.

Everyone would be healthy in spirit, soul, and body. Obesity, disease, and sickness would disappear along with shame, anxiety, and fear.

Love would be the rule of law. Jesus would be the center of attention, and worship would be awesome.

Freedom would reign.

Jesus is fully committed to not violating anyone's free will and working with the church to make earth like heaven.

So, what part do you want to help with? You don't have to do everything, just something. Jesus has all authority in heaven and on earth, and He wants to delegate a little to you.

Sure, there is still plenty of territory to possess, and some fighting left to take it, but what else is there to do? You were born for this. God has a specific area that He made you perfect for, will you accept the challenge?

DAY 51: Joshua 14 - 17

Give Me This Mountain!

Now therefore, give me this mountain of which the LORD spoke in that day.

I love Caleb.

What an excellent example for us to emulate.

He was one of the original spies sent to check out the promised land, and along with Joshua, gave a good report.

I think what I love about him most is his perspective. He was so ambitious, tenacious and persistent-- and his courage was legendary.

Caleb believed that wholly following the Lord meant being aggressive, optimistic, ambitious, and passionate about his inheritance.

He thought his desires were good and didn't mind picking a fight to get them.

Hebron, a city on a hill where Abraham buried Sarah and David was later named king, became his inheritance.

It used to be called Kirjath Arba, after Arba the greatest of all the giants.

But not anymore.

Now it's called Caleb's backyard, and his grandkids play where those giants used to scare the pants off of every soldier walking up that hill.

What if believers are supposed to be bold and ambitious like Caleb?

Maybe what we call "waiting on God" is actually wandering around in the wilderness of fear and regret, and we should be saying, "give me this mountain!"

DAY 52: Joshua 18 - 21

Your Last Name Is Good

How long will you neglect to go and possess the land which the LORD God of your fathers has given you?

Like the retinas in your eyes and the fingerprints on your hands, you have a unique purpose and identity.

Discovering it is fascinating and comes from an ongoing relationship with your Father that is so much fun.

But that process is for those who are growing up and coming into their own.

You don't want to start there.

If you try to understand who you are by starting with your first name (what makes you unique), instead of your last name (what makes you belong), then you will never fully understand.

The Father adopted you into His family, and you belong there. You have your Father's likeness through the work of Jesus, and His nature is GOOD.

Therefore, your last name is GOOD.

Whatever your first name turns out to be, you can be sure of your last. Your DNA is GOOD. Your nature is GOOD. Your heart is GOOD. Your inheritance is GOOD. Your family history is GOOD. Your identity is GOOD.

You have no pre-existing conditions. You are completely safe. You belong. There is plenty to go around.

So RELAX and BREATHE and REST in the fact that you are a part of the family. Your Papa is God.

DAY 53: Joshua 22 - Judges 1

Daddy's Girl

So she said to him, "Give me a blessing; since you have given me land in the South, give me also springs of water." And Caleb gave her the upper springs and the lower springs.

Achsah was having a big day.

She was about to get married to the strongest and bravest man around, who had just conquered a stronghold to win her hand.

She inherited a beautiful piece of property to call her own and begin her new life. Her Daddy was happy, her groom to be was smiling, and she was delighted.

As she trotted up to her future husband on her donkey, she thought, "I know my Dad, he's beaming right now. He's the 'Give me this mountain' guy who is passionate to the max. I've got to tell Othniel to ask for more."

Jumping down from her donkey, surrounded by her father, her fiance', and the other warriors, she exudes confidence.

Caleb smiles and says, "What would you like?"

"Since you are giving me this land, give me springs of water to go with it."

So Caleb gave Achsah the upper and lower springs.

Your life is changing for the better. You are coming into your inheritance, understanding your identity, and becoming fruitful. Good stuff is happening, so don't settle for less than you want.

Father, I know you, and I want to be just like you. While you are blessing me with new relationships, a new identity, a new job, and all these other things, bless me with one more thing. I want my own source of water. I want a connection with Holy Spirit so I can hear You for myself.

DAY 54: Judges 2 - 5

No Longer Neutral

And it came to pass, when the judge was dead, that they returned, and corrupted themselves more than their fathers.

Remember the old teeter-totters?

Always going back and forth, up and down, and hoping that the guy on the other side didn't jump off and leave you crashing to the ground.

Most Christians are under the misguided impression that their heart is like that, a neutral playground where the heaviest kid wins.

How about the tired angel on one shoulder, demon on the other picture?

We think that our hearts are the neutral territory for some negotiation between a good guy and a bag guy, and whoever we agree with wins.

Then there's the white dog, black dog analogy. Again, we're a neutral field, could go either way-- it's all about which one you feed and which one you starve. Yikes.

The book of Judges personifies this neutral heart concept. When a good leader arose, Israel excelled, but when they died, it was back to the same old nonsense.

But the good news of the gospel is this-- your heart is not neutral. The Holy Spirit doesn't play on a neutral playground. He completely guts your sin nature and builds a spectacular secret garden in its place.

Your heart is GOOD, not neutral. You are not an experiment God is running; you are a son or daughter that He is loving. As soon as you believe that you're a child of God, not an orphan, you will start working with Him, and the game will change completely.

DAY 55: Judges 6 - 9

You Mighty Man Of Valor

And the Angel of the LORD appeared to him, and said to him, "The LORD is with you, you mighty man of valor!"

Where are all the miracles when you need one?

I bet you have heard someone say something like that, or maybe you have said it yourself.

We love the idea of the damsel in distress being rescued from the bad guy by the knight in shining armor riding in on the white horse. As long as we are the damsel, that is.

But God is not interested in a castle full of helpless victims, barely saved "by the grace of God." He wants you to think of yourself as a mighty man of valor.

Miracles don't go to those who need them; they go to the mighty ones, the people who will believe God and act with courage when He speaks.

I know, I know. I hear all of the arguments out there. What about the little girl lying dead in the room, she needs a miracle and can't become mighty without it. I get it.

But even when the little girl is helpless, someone had to go in faith and get Jesus (a mighty man of valor.) When God wants to respond to a need, answer a prayer, or rescue the helpless, He does it by inviting a Gideon to think of themselves as a mighty man.

So, how will you respond?

Someone needs you to respond, to think of yourself as mighty. Can you hear the Lord saying to you, "Go in this might of yours, and you shall save ________________ from ________________. Have I not sent you?"

DAY 56: Judges 10 - 13

Raising World Changers

"O my Lord, please let the Man of God whom You sent come to us again and teach us what we shall do for the child who will be born."

Samson's parents asked a brilliant question.

The Angel of the Lord appeared to his mother, pronouncing how unique Samson would be, and then left.

She told her husband what happened, and so he prayed, "God, please don't just give me a prophecy; tell me specific instructions about how to raise a child like this."

So the Angel returned with detailed instructions that were critical to Samson's success.

Now that's good parenting. If you are trying to raise world changers, pay careful attention to their example.

Every prophecy should be followed by the prayer, "Please teach me how to do what you just said was going to happen."

Every word has a specific set of instructions that accompany it, and unless we ask, we may miss it.

I remember when my first born son was still a baby and very fussy, and we were not getting much sleep. He was sensitive, and I was exasperated.

Then the Lord woke me up and said two words to me, "ENJOY HIM." That was many years ago, but I still remember, and those two words have made an enormous difference in our lives. Take a minute and think about your kids. What are their prophetic words? Perhaps it would help to pray, "Please teach me how to raise a child like this."

DAY 57: Judges 14 - 17

Not Ordinary

If I be shaven, then my strength will go from me, and I shall become weak, and be like any other man.

Ordinary. Just like any other man. Those words had to hurt coming out of Samson's mouth. Delilah nagged him to the point that he couldn't take it anymore, so he revealed everything to her. He told her the secret to making him just like any other man.

The Anointing of the Holy Spirit is what made Samson extraordinary, giving him a kind of superpower that he was supposed to use to deliver his people from their oppressors.

The Anointing of the Holy Spirit is what makes you and I extraordinary as well, imparting gifts to make the world a better place. Without Him, we are just ordinary men and women.

With Him, however, we are powerful. We are world changers, people builders, disease healers, problem solvers, and champions of courage. **He is the secret to our strength.**

We must protect our relationship with the Holy Spirit above all else. But like Samson, anxiety, stress, and numbness from giving in to lesser desires chips away at our souls. We should be pursuing the BIG desire God has put inside of us, the superpower we have that will change the world. Instead, we let the little weeds choke out the fruit tree.

Protect your superpower above all else by keeping your focus on your relationship with the Holy Spirit. Refuse to give in to the weak little desires that distract you from the ONE BIG DESIRE that God put inside of you.

If you feel the drip, drip, drip of nagging wearing you down, get up! Don't give up the secret to your power, protect it at all costs.

DAY 58: Judges 18 - 21

The Heart Of The King

In those days there was no king in Israel; everyone did what was right in his own eyes.

Running wild and free through the countryside doing whatever I please-- no boss, no government, no one telling me what to do.

Utopia. Anarchy. Everyone was living for "love," doing what was right in their own eyes. How does that sound? **Terrifying.**

Jesus saw us like that, scattered and isolated, like sheep without a shepherd, and compassion moved Him to action. Why? Because your heart longs to belong and your mind needs to connect. You were born to be led, not by just anyone, but by THE KING.

King Jesus stands alone-- no one even comes close to the standard He sets. He is the one and only.

- Who else would sacrifice Himself to save His people?
- Who else would develop a personal relationship with every person He leads?
- Who else would make us family, taking personal responsibility for all?
- Who else would keep our best interest top priority, so we can fully trust Him?
- Who else would connect us with power, grace, revelation, and peace through the Spirit?
- Who else could introduce us to the Creator as Sons and Daughters?
- Who else would keep open communication with billions of people at once?
- Who else would inspire greatness in every man, woman, and child?
- Who else could secure our future forever, so we never have to fear death?
- Who else cares like Him, leads like Him, and empowers like Him?

There is no other KING like Jesus.

DAY 59: Ruth 1 - 4

Pursuing Prosperity

May you prosper in Ephrathah and be famous in Bethlehem.

Should Christians pursue prosperity? It's kind of a trick question.

Am I asking if we should pursue independence from God, greed, or self-centeredness? Of course not.

But I am asking questions like this:

Should Christians have average marriages or amazing ones?
Should we seek to be the best employee at our job or settle for middle of the pack?
Should we start businesses and follow growth strategies?
Should Christians tithe 10% of their income and give generously on top of that?
Should we produce life-changing books, inspiring songs, and great works of art?
Should we solve big problems like racism, poverty, disease, and divorce?
Should we leave an inheritance for our children and grandchildren?
Should we pursue personal growth and higher education?
Should we get involved in politics, government, and the community and try to make life better?
Should we spread the gospel throughout the world?
Should we teach our children to change the world and disciple nations?
Should we pray "Your Kingdom come, on earth as it is in heaven?"
Should we strive for healthy bodies and minds, or settle for mediocrity?

I think you would agree that the answer to those questions is a resounding YES.

Real prosperity comes from following the principles of the scripture, pursuing excellence, mastering our craft, loving others, adding value to society, and seeking first the kingdom.

DAY 60: 1 Samuel 1 - 4

Training Your Senses

"Speak, for Your servant hears."

You can LEARN to recognize His voice.

I am never going to be an Olympic level sprinter; I am just not built that way. I can get better at it, but at my very best I will only be an average sprinter. Talent matters, gifts matter, and natural ability matters.

It is the same in the Kingdom. God made us all unique so that we need each other and can build each other up.

But life is about 20% talent and about 80% practice and growth.

Our job, with the help of those around us, is two-fold: recognizing what God gives us and growing those gifts to maximize their potential.

Here are a few things that will help you reach your maximum potential.

FOCUS. Paul told Timothy to give himself entirely to the gifts that he received so his progress would be evident to all.

GET A COACH. Samuel dedicated himself to the Lord, but he still needed the guidance and experience that Eli provided.

PRACTICE. Hebrews 5 tells us that we mature in our gifts by trial and error, or practice.

ADOPT A GROWTH MINDSET. If you believe you can learn to do something, then you will put forth the effort to do so, but if you think that God predetermines every detail of your life, you will never try.

CARE ABOUT PEOPLE. If you adopt God's mission to love people into wholeness, then He will provide what you need to succeed.

DAY 61: 1 Samuel 5 - 8

So Far

Then Samuel took a stone and set it up between Mizpah and Shen, and called its name Ebenezer, saying, "Thus far the LORD has helped us."

So, you have repented of your orphan thinking and started feeling like a Son or Daughter. You no longer have a divided heart, you're pursuing the will of the Lord. You fasted, prayed, and gave up the stuff holding you back, and now you are ready to move forward!

Taking the fight to the enemy, you get back some of the ground he has held in your life for a long time. YES! But then the voice of doubt tries to creep in.

"It's not like you changed the world."

"Sure, you made a little progress, but look how far you have left to go."

"You're doing fine in that area, but remember all of those other areas you are lagging in."

"What about the BIG promise that you are still waiting on-- that's never going to happen."

The voice of doubt would love to get in your head and drag you back into slavery, but NOT THIS TIME! Like Samuel, you have learned something, and you're not going to forget it. So, you do what he did; you erect a memorial stone at the forward position of your breakthrough that says, "SO FAR THE LORD HAS HELPED ME."

"I may not have everything I want yet, but I have won a real victory. I am not going to forget this breakthrough, nor am I ever going back. So far the Lord has helped me, and if He has helped me this far, He will help me finish the job."

DAY 62: 1 Samuel 9 - 12

Identity vs. Anointing

And the LORD answered, "There he is, hidden among the equipment."

What an incredible start Saul had. Samuel read his mail with such clarity there was no doubt, and every sign Samuel predicted came true.

But he was not usually this kind of guy. He didn't think of himself as brave, as a leader, or as a prophet. But this whole Anointing thing was awesome.

With God resting on him he was a different person.

The WORD of the LORD, the CONFIDENCE of the prophet, the SIGNS that came true, and the FEELING of courage that came with the Anointing helped him do what he would have never even tried before.

But it had to be a fluke, right? Saul thought of himself as a good son and a hard worker; but a King, no way. He couldn't even talk about what Samuel said to his dad, and when it was time for him to be King, he hid in the equipment.

His identity was not Kingly. In his heart, he was not confident, decisive, brave, or well spoken.

The Anointing is amazing, but it doesn't last. He overshadows you when the need arises and then lifts when the mission is accomplished, leaving you as, well, just you.

When you're laying in your bed alone, the way you think about yourself is all that matters.

IDENTITY always wins in the end. Your ability to be alone with God, loving Him and feeling his love, and living humble, grateful, and confident is what defines you.

DAY 63: 1 Samuel 13 - 16

Living With Favor

And the LORD said, "Arise, anoint him; for this is the one!"

The most respected man in the country was at his house, and David was mowing the grass (yeah, I know, he was watching the sheep-- same thing.)

He was the youngest, but he was THE ONE. He caught the attention of the only One whose opinion mattered. Most of us are used to being treated like the youngest, not respected, or ignored. That was how others felt about David too.

But that was not how David felt about himself-- not even close. Unlike Saul, when the Spirit of God came upon David it did not turn him into another man, it enhanced who he already was, a man after God's heart.

What would it be like to be the "Beloved Son in whom He is well pleased?" How would it feel to be the Anointed of the Lord, the "Man After God's own heart?"

What if your circumstances don't determine your courage, but your courage determines your circumstances? What if you lived with such an abandoned heart that God couldn't help but favor you?

Listen to the description of David by one of Saul's servants, "Look, I have seen a son of Jesse the Bethlehemite, who is skillful in playing, a mighty man of valor, a man of war, prudent in speech, and a handsome person; and the LORD is with him." He developed that kind of IDENTITY when no one else thought of him that way, and when the Spirit of the Lord came on him, it magnified what God already knew was there.

Why couldn't that be you? You could think of yourself as a king, a warrior, a great communicator, a skillful artist, and good looking before anyone knows your name.

DAY 64: 1 Samuel 17 - 20

Necessity

Then David spoke to the men who stood by him, saying, "What shall be done for the man who kills this Philistine and takes away the reproach from Israel?

World changers think differently than everyone else. They feel obligated to make things better-- it's almost as if they have to. Why are they compelled to act when everyone else is running scared? They weren't born that way, and they face challenges like every other person on the planet.

Motivation is not a habit you set in motion and then let run in the background; you must create it every day. David was the champion of necessity. He had to intervene; there was no other choice. Here are some reasons why David went after Goliath that we can use to face our giants.

THERE IS A JUST CAUSE. If you can see a problem, you are the person to solve it.

PEOPLE ARE COUNTING ON YOU. Love is the best motivator.

YOU KNOW YOU CAN HELP. If you put forth your best effort and believed God for supernatural help, could you make a difference? Then you should act.

THERE IS A BIG REWARD.

IT'S JUST WHO YOU ARE. You are the kind of person who seeks out challenges, adds value to others, loves well, and makes a difference.

TO PROTECT OUR REPUTATION. Nothing will defy my friends, family, and community and get away with it.

TO HONOR THE LORD. Would it honor the Lord more if you sat there and watched, or if you joined the fight?

DAY 65: 1 Samuel 21 - 24

You Can't Hide Awesome

"As the proverb of the ancients says, 'Wickedness proceeds from the wicked.'

Your identity will ALWAYS overpower circumstances given enough time-- you can't hide WHO YOU ARE.

Saul was insecure at his core. He never thought of himself as kingly, and he caused a self-sabotaging pattern to prove it. His insecurity made him disobey God to gain the favor of the people, and God rejected him as king because of it. That rejection produced more instability, and the pattern continued.

David, on the other hand, was a king at heart. He thought of himself as a leader, warrior, communicator, and man of God. No matter what circumstance he encountered his inner strength rose to the surface.

You can't hide who you are, but you can change how you think. You can throw off your old identity and adopt the one God has for you, but it will not happen accidentally. To change the way you think about yourself, follow these steps:

Repent for your orphan thinking. Orphan thinking is the root of all sin, and you must ruthlessly eliminate it.

Get clarity about who God says you are. Take the time to search the scriptures and your testimonies, desires, and prophetic words until you get a clear picture of how He sees you.

Change the way you talk to and about yourself. Talk to yourself like you would coach someone else.

Change who you listen to. Find friends and mentors who place a demand on your true identity and teach you how to get there.

DAY 66: 1 Samuel 25 - 28

Peacemaker

Please forgive the trespass of your maidservant. For the LORD will certainly make for my lord an enduring house, because my lord fights the battles of the LORD, and evil is not found in you throughout your days."

No one determines your identity except you and God.

Your heart is your own, to tend and keep like a secret garden for the Lord to enjoy.

It's your job to develop confidence, happiness, and the desire for greatness.

No one else can do it for you, and no one can stop you.

Confident, beautiful, and wise, Abigail was a perfect example of this.

She was married to a guy named FOOL, yet she cultivated her heart into something completely different.

Her timely words of wisdom and generosity saved her entire household from disaster.

She was a peacemaker, and God blessed her for it.

But things could have been very different. If Abigail did not take responsibility for her heart and cultivate it into good soil, she would have been a victim with the rest.

Tend the garden of your heart and make it God's favorite place to plant His ideas.

You will bear fruit eventually.

DAY 67: 1 Samuel 29 - 2 Samuel 1

Strengthening Yourself

But David strengthened himself in the LORD his God.

Eventually disappointment will slap you in the face. Something completely unfair will happen, beyond your control, and you will face the raw emotion and paralyzing numbness of grief.

A big fat WHY will hover over you while BLAME circles around trying to kill your momentum. You are not the kind of person who allows emotion to rule your life, but these are some strong feelings. What are you going to do?

You are going to strengthen yourself in the Lord.

Here's how to do it:

CRY. Let yourself feel the emotion of the moment and deeply grieve your loss. Don't skip this.
BREATHE. Find some space to be alone and breathe, then regain your composure.
REMEMBER. Take the time to remember a time when God helped you before and a promise about your future.
TALK TO YOURSELF. You've got this. God helped you before, and He will do it again. You have a bright future. You are the anointed of the Lord, His favorite. It's not over yet.
SING. Find a song or Psalm that expresses your heart and sing it out loud with energy. Singing releases emotions better than anything else.
GET UP. Stand up strong in the identity the Lord has given you.
PRAY. Don't just pray a general prayer-- ask for specifics about what you can do to make this right.
ACT. Take specific and decisive action that demonstrates the following: you're not a victim, you're confident God is with you, you know who you are, you remember your testimonies, you believe your promises, and you know others are counting on you.

DAY 68: 2 Samuel 2 - 5

David's Secret To Success

So David inquired of the LORD.

If you read through the life of David, you will see these words often: "So David inquired of the LORD." At every major decision point of his life, David asked God what to do. It was a habit that he formed early and repeated often.

On the surface, it appears similar to what most of us do. We are all intrigued with what "the will of God" is for our lives, and it is common for us to inquire about it. But if you dig a little deeper, you discover that the inquiring that David did was different.

David BELIEVED that he was the anointed of the Lord, the warrior who fought God's battles, and the king who should lead His people. He was not approaching God for affirmation; he already had it.

David was AMBITIOUS. He wanted to grow, fight, win, lead, and prosper. He was not approaching God for motivation; he was full of it.

David ENJOYED life and was emotionally whole. He was not approaching God for healing; he already had a way to stay strong emotionally.

David approached God with the longing to do what God called him to do, inquiring about specific direction. He wanted to understand the timing, strategy, and personnel details that only the Lord could know so he could WIN, and he followed the Lord's directions precisely.

David assumed that God liked him, called him, and wanted him to succeed because God had already said those things.

We must believe our Father and intentionally cultivate confidence, happiness, and ambition BEFORE we inquire about the details of His will or we will waste the ideas God gives us.

DAY 69: 2 Samuel 6 - 9

His Presence Comes First

So David and all the house of Israel brought up the ark of the LORD with shouting and with the sound of the trumpet.

Building confidence on the inside so that you KNOW you are a Son or Daughter of the King is step one.

Cultivating emotional wholeness in your heart so that you live HAPPY and free of fear, anger, shame, and insecurity is step two.

Creating desire within you so that you live with the ambition to be GREAT is step three.

With those things in place, you are ready to hear the voice of God and grow fruitful ministries, businesses, relationships, families, cities, schools, and projects.

But that is not the goal, that is the foundation from which we reach for it.

There is only one thing that matters, HOSTING GOD'S PRESENCE.

Everything we do is for ONE THING, to build a dwelling place for God.

Oh, that we would become OBSESSED like David with the ONLY thing that matters, to build a culture around the Presence.

Lift your vision higher! Give yourself entirely to the ONE THING.

Enough with the orphan thinking, brokenness, and apathy. It's time to be who you were created to be so that God's glory can rest on you.

ONE THING I HAVE DESIRED OF THE LORD, AND THAT WILL I SEEK.

DAY 70: 2 Samuel 10 - 13

Prosperity vs. Greed

"I also would have given you much more!"

David had it all: anointing, favor, riches, power, authority, family, talent, and good looks. But it did not start that way.

He began with a sense of identity, a heart for worship, courage to fight the Lord's battles, a genuine desire to know God's will, an obedient spirit, and a willingness to lead. Those things attracted God to him, and over time caused him to prosper.

God wanted David to flourish.

The attributes that caused David to gain prosperity--his loyalty, courage, devotion, obedience, and leadership--were deeply rooted in his identity. As long as he stayed true to that identity and SERVED THE LORD, then blessings followed.

"No one can serve two masters," Jesus said. Your devotion must remain with the LORD, serving His agenda to add value to others. You can't retain the right to control if the LORD is your Master.

But the opposite of serving the Lord is not prosperity; it's greed and selfishness. Greed says, "I don't care about the identity the Lord gave me, adding value to others, or waiting to bear fruit-- I want it now without the process."

Use your confidence, happiness, and ambition to SERVE THE LORD and ADD VALUE TO OTHERS, and you will prosper. The better you get at it, the more you will gain.

But like David, if you lose sight of your purpose, stop adding value, and start taking from God's people, your divided heart will steal away the very things that produce your prosperity.

DAY 71: 2 Samuel 14 - 17

Devising Means

Yet God does not take away a life; but He devises means, so that His banished ones are not expelled from Him.

Love is, by nature, GENEROUS, demonstrating to all that there is always more. Love initiates action from a place of abundance. It is the antonym of poverty. What God does, and therefore what love does, is devise means to get the desired result. Love assumes that there is always MORE, always ENOUGH, always a way. It is creative and energetic, never limited or restrained.

When God desired the voluntary fellowship of a people capable of genuine love, He created the world and made man in His image. After people chose to live like orphans, God figured out a way through Jesus to bring them back into fellowship. When He desired to bring His people out of slavery in Egypt, He devised a plan that included calling a leader, parting the sea, appearing in a cloud, and initiating a relationship.

Love finds a way to get what it wants that is both legal and beneficial to everyone involved. In contrast, poverty operates from a limited supply, assuming there is only so much to go around.

Poverty says, "We can't afford that," while Love says, "How can we afford that?"
Poverty says, "There's no way," while Love says, "How can we get this done?"
Poverty says, "We have to separate," while Love says, "How can we make this work?"
Poverty says, "I don't have time," while Love says, "How can I make time?"
Poverty says, "I don't have the energy," while Love says, "How can I generate more energy?"

LOVE devises means, creates more, generates energy, assumes abundance, and finds a way.

DAY 72: 2 Samuel 18 - 21

Giant Killers

These four were born to the giant in Gath, and fell by the hand of David and by the hand of his servants.

The breeze blowing in his hair as he played and sang sweet music before the Lord, David's young mind would often drift to greatness. He remembered the day when the lion went down by his bare hands, the oil dripping down his head as Samuel proclaimed him the next king, and the victorious struggle with the bear.

Finally, after many nights alone in the field with his music, the sheep, and the presence of the Lord, David killed Goliath. He won a victory so big that it inspired the entire nation.

Many years later, when David was getting too old to fight, those around him were still killing giants. Four of Goliath's sons went down by the hand of David's family or friends.

There are giants left in the land. Poverty, racism, cancer, abortion, diabetes, sexual immorality, divorce, and addiction are all defying the people of God.

You could do something about that. Right now you may have a lion or a bear staring you down just asking to be conquered. Maybe it's your weight, lack, health, relationships, or undeveloped skills.

Get up and defeat that thing! All you need is CONFIDENCE, WHOLENESS, and DESIRE, and you can cultivate them.

This world is begging for a CULTURE OF GIANT KILLERS to manifest in the land. That will not happen unless YOU win some personal battles and then pick a fight with a giant.

DAY 73: 2 Samuel 22 - 1 Kings 1

A Mighty Generation

These are the names of the mighty men whom David had...

A few years earlier there were two swords in the entire nation of Israel, one for Saul and one for Jonathan. A handful of soldiers surrounded Saul doing nothing, while the rest of the nation hid from the enemy.

Now there were over a million fully equipped warriors ready to fight, and every enemy was defeated.

There were so many mighty men that David ranked them according to their ridiculous accomplishments. One guy killed 800 men at one time! Another chased a lion down into his den and killed it. **What happened in those few years that changed the culture so drastically?**

God didn't change. He was the same God who delivered them from Egypt and many enemies since. Genetics had not changed. It was the same families living in the same cities and farms that had produced these men.

Necessity had not changed. The same enemy that was oppressing them before was getting pounded now. There was no change in nutrition, the priesthood, the covenant, timing, the favor of God, or education.

So what made the difference?

David.

One guy with a BIG IDENTITY, extraordinary focus on the PRESENCE OF GOD, WILLINGNESS TO LEAD, and the LONGING TO FIGHT AND WIN THE LORD'S BATTLES changed everything in one generation.

DAY 74: 1 Kings 2 - 5

An Understanding Heart

At Gibeon the LORD appeared to Solomon in a dream by night; and God said, "Ask! What shall I give you?"

Everything prospers as your heart prospers.

Solomon knew this perhaps better than anyone.

He said in one of his Proverbs, "To him who has understanding, knowledge is easy."

In other words, if your heart is tender and fertile, receiving information from heaven and growing it is normal. Knowing HOW to do anything becomes as simple as placing a seed in the ground and watching it grow.

Want to know how to lead a nation, raise a family, grow a church, prosper in business, or get healthy? No problem. There is an answer to every question, a better way to do anything.

The ONLY limiting factor is the condition of the heart.

Do you want a receptive heart? If you do, follow Solomon's example.

Get God's attention with your gratitude, then just ask.

Receive it by faith, take responsibility for it, and start cultivating it.

Build your confidence, happiness, and ambition while you anticipate the words of wisdom from heaven. When they come, your tender heart will receive them, and everything in your life will prosper.

DAY 75: 1 Kings 6 - 9

Extravagant Desire

When Solomon had finished building the house of the LORD and the king's house, and all Solomon's desire which he wanted to do...

Desire is such a critical part of the Christian life, but it worries us like an embarrassing relative at a family function. "DESIRE? Is that even Christian? Just do your best, wait your turn, serve, give, and hang in there."

"I just want what God wants; I want to do His will, whatever that is." When we say things like that, we imply eking out a meager existence and enduring difficult circumstances. Somehow "God's will" for every Christian is to survive while we build our "character."

Solomon must have missed that lesson growing up in David's house because he wanted some fantastic stuff. He built the most exquisite building on the planet not because God told him to, but because he wanted to.

And you know what? GOD LOVED IT. God appeared to him and said, "I have heard your prayer and your supplication that you have made before Me; I have consecrated this house which you have built to put My name there forever, and My eyes and My heart will be there perpetually." That's pretty cool.

I'm looking forward to the day that the conversations at church sound like this:

"I want to write a bestselling book and start a movement."
"I want to get my Ph.D. and discover the cure for cancer."
"I want to build a world-class business."
"I want to raise some kids who change the world."
"I want to break the power of addiction in my region."

DAY 76: 1 Kings 10 - 13

Loyalty

Solomon did evil in the sight of the LORD, and did not fully follow the LORD, as did his father David.

Solomon was the wealthiest man on the planet. His wisdom was legendary; the way he built, designed, managed, organized, and led left the Queen of Sheba breathless. All of it was from God and for God--until it wasn't. Over the years he lost his way, his heart, his loyalty.

God had no problem with his prosperity and wisdom; He was the one that gave Solomon those things. But God did have a problem with Solomon's heart drifted from loyal devotion to embracing other gods. Abundance did not cause Solomon's loyalty problem; we know that because David remained faithful to the end even as he prospered. **So what caused his heart to drift?**

We know from Jesus that all evil comes from within, from the way we think about ourselves in our hearts. Solomon began to think of himself as bulletproof, and he ignored the warnings of the Lord. He married women that were loyal to other gods, and that divided loyalty ended up costing him and the nation dearly.

It's ALL ABOUT THE RELATIONSHIP. I would have no problem if my wife prospered-- in fact, I would love it. As her wealth, wisdom, fitness, friendships, and health increased, the better it would make me feel. There is only one thing that would cause a problem-- if her heart turned to another man.

God is the same way. He is not a vending machine where we slip in our prayers and get answers out. It is all about the relationship to Him, developing trust, love, and loyalty in a mutual romance.

DAY 77: 1 Kings 14 - 17

When The Brook Dries Up

And it happened after a while that the brook dried up, because there had been no rain in the land.

Abundance flows like a river when there is a noble king, but that was not the case in Israel.

Elijah stood in his Ahab's face and proclaimed there would be no rain for three years except at his word, and then it was time to hide.

The Lord sent him to a brook that he drank from while ravens fed him twice a day. It was a good set up until the water dried up.

From his mouth came the proclamation of no rain, and now he had nothing to drink. He wasn't doing anything wrong; something was just not right.

Elijah was the good guy, Ahab and Jezebel were the problems. Prophets are supposed to support Kings and Queens that bring prosperity to the nation, but these guys were the worst.

Through no fault of his own, while trying to do the right thing, his provision dries up. What do I do now?

Leave Israel, go to a widow and her son's house, and add value to them. So Elijah went.

They were a blessing to him, and he was a Godsend to that family.

No matter what, in any circumstance, **there is always someone to whom you can add value**, and provision always follows those who bless others.

DAY 78: 1 Kings 18 - 21

You Are Not Alone

Then Elijah said to the people, "I alone am left a prophet of the LORD; but Baal's prophets are four hundred and fifty men.

Jesus said, "I did not come to condemn the world, but that the world through me might be saved." In Elijah's day, things were a little different. His job, because of the stubbornness of the king and queen, was to proclaim judgment. He was to announce warnings knowing that they would not heed them so God could judge their wickedness.

He did that job faithfully, hearing the voice of the Lord and acting in obedience as well anyone has. His spirit and power are legendary.

When that same spirit and power rested on John the Baptist in the days of Jesus as prophesied by Malachi, the results were incomparable. The same anointing that had ruined a kingdom in Elijah's day was now "turning the hearts of fathers to sons." The same spirit was bringing reconciliation.

WHY? Because there was a solution now, not just a problem. In the time of Elijah, only the problem existed, there was no way to turn a bad heart good. But Jesus changed all that.

If we're not careful, our faith lingers back in the past, causing us to believe the world is getting worse and there is nothing we can do about it. We feel alone, and we end up depressed. However, that's not the case at all. We are the kings and queens, discipling nations through the power of the Holy Spirit.

Guard yourself against the temptation to drift back into judgment mode. You are not alone. There are hundreds of millions of like-minded, Spirit-filled believers who love Jesus with all of their hearts.

DAY 79: 1 Kings 22 - 2 Kings 3

Give Me Double

Elisha said, "Please let a double portion of your spirit be upon me."

Christian ambition. Those words don't seem to fit together in the same sentence, do they? We typically associate Christian virtues with humility, contentment, self-control, and patience-- and we should. The example of Jesus and the teaching of the New Testament uphold these values as critical.

But as we read through the Scriptures, we keep running into people like Elisha, whose heart's desire was to have double of what the most anointed man on the planet had. **Sounds ambitious to me.**

Abraham walked across the land claiming every place he set foot on for his family. David asked, "What shall be done for the man who defeats this giant who defies the army of the living God?"

Solomon built ships to scour the earth for treasure, making silver as common as stones in Israel. Jesus stood up in town after town saying, "I am the Anointed Savior you have all been waiting for."

The disciples argued about who would be the greatest. The Apostle Paul boasted of preaching the Gospel to entire provinces.

So which is it, ambition or contentment? Jesus said that a fruitful person is one who learns how to prepare his or her heart, recognize when a desire is from the Lord, grow that desire into something big, and then bear fruit with patience. **It's not one or the other; it's both.**

Ambition is not the enemy, control is. Jesus wants you to want more, but you have to do things His way.

DAY 80: 2 Kings 4 - 7

The Notable Woman

Now it happened one day that Elisha went to Shunem, where there was a notable woman, and she persuaded him to eat some food.

I love the story of the NOTABLE WOMAN, and I love how she got Elisha's attention. She was famous, but it wasn't wealth that got everyone's attention. The woman did not have any children, nor does it seem that she worked in any unique field of interest. She was notable because she had a great attitude, was thoughtful and kind, and hosted people well. **Her communication skills made her stand out.**

A high value for both the anointing and the prophet of God caused her to go above and beyond caring for Elisha, and it got God's attention. She wasn't in it for the reward, but you can't out give God. Everything was fine when she loved others, but now God messed with the longings of her heart and promised her a son.

"Don't you dare get my hopes up about something like that, it's too dear to my heart. You can't promise me the longing of my heart unless you are going to DELIVER ON YOUR PROMISE."

Ever felt like that? You are going along fine, trying your best to be the kind of person you think you should be, then God messes it all up with a promise.

"Why can't you leave my heart alone and let me serve? I finally got to the place I can live without the crushing weight of hope, and now you stir it up again."

But God is not nervous. He is MORE THAN ABLE to do above all that we can ask or think, but He wants you to anticipate it before it happens.

DAY 81: 2 Kings 8 - 11

Brutally Honest

Then he said, "Throw her down."

Dust swirled in the air as the chariot closed the distance to the city.

"Who is that?" someone asked. "I'm not sure, but he drives like a crazy person. It must be Jehu-- this can't be good."

It wasn't good. The time had come for the house of Ahab and Jezebel to reap what they had sown, and God had chosen the right man for the job.

Jehu was ruthless. Peacetime is for the meek, but this assignment required zeal, and Jehu was a man of swift and decisive force.

He quickly dealt with those who tried to resist, recruited the willing to his side, and then came to where Jezebel was staying. With one question and one command, the whole thing was over.

"Who is on my side?" he asked the men standing with Jezebel. A couple of guys looked out at him. "Throw her down."

That was it, game over.

No longer is our fight with flesh and blood; we struggle to believe the truth.

As you renew your mind, you will run into thinking patterns that reek of an orphan mindset. You must take responsibility for your heart and deal with victim thinking ruthlessly.

Don't be gentle-- throw those old mindsets down with brutal honesty as you pledge your loyalty to Jesus and Kingdom thinking.

DAY 82: 2 Kings 12 - 15

Don't Settle

You should have struck five or six times; then you would have struck Syria till you had destroyed it!

Grace is beginning to flow into your life-- you can feel it.

Not much has changed on the outside, but something is different.

God is speaking to your heart more often, stirring up hope. The desire for more is bubbling up, creating enough hunger to unsettle you.

Finally, you get a breakthrough. The wind begins to fill your sails, and you feel something you haven't felt in a long time-- **momentum.**

You could be grateful for what you have and go back to normal; that's what you have always done before.

Your life isn't that bad.

Your history taps you on the shoulder to remind you that you're not that special-- maybe you should settle.

You are doing better than most of your friends.

A still, small voice deep inside calls out, "Complete deliverance is available. Freedom from every oppressor is there for the taking, so take it. You were born for greatness; keep going, keep believing. **Don't settle**."

WHAT ARE YOU GOING TO DO?

DAY 83: 2 Kings 16 - 19

Whole

For he held fast to the LORD; he did not depart from following Him, but kept His commandments.

Wholeness is the state in which you relate to the Father with confidence, are healed from every wound, and experience genuine happiness.

It is living with one big desire that swallows up all the petty little desires trying to steal your attention.

Being whole means living undivided and putting all of your trust in the one and only God.

The goal is to get your happy and healthy heart in perfect alignment with God's purpose for your life-- **that's the sweet spot.**

Hezekiah found it, and he prospered in all that he did.

Jesus walked in it, referring to it as "My peace."

My prayer for you today is that you experience the wholeness Paul talks about in 1 Thessalonians 5:23:

"Now may the God of peace Himself sanctify you completely; and may your whole spirit, soul, and body be preserved blameless at the coming of our Lord Jesus Christ."

DAY 84: 2 Kings 20 - 23

Facing The Wall

Then he turned his face toward the wall, and prayed to the LORD.

Consider Hezekiah's predicament.

Isaiah the prophet, possibly the most accurate predictor of the future in the Old Testament, walks into Hezekiah's house while he is sick. Looking him dead in the face, Isaiah tells Hezekiah the word of the Lord, "Get your house in order, you're going to die."

The will of the Lord is crystal clear at this point, right?

Hezekiah turns towards the wall and begins to weep. "O Lord, remember how I have walked before you in truth and loyalty." Before Isaiah could get out of the courtyard God spoke to him-- God was going to heal the King and add 15 years to his life.

Now, was God lying, did Hezekiah's tears change God's mind, or was God trying to draw Hezekiah's faith to the surface in the first place? The answer to that question is a little above my pay grade, but I suspect the latter.

You are not on a raft floating along on the river of God's will with your only options staying in or getting out-- that's not how life works.

The will of God for your life is for you to understand the identity He gave you, develop your confidence, happiness, and focus, and then bear fruit as He speaks to you.

Hezekiah's genuine tears and confident cry came from a life lived for God, and **the will of God for him was to respond like a son.** He did so, God loved it, and changed the plan.

DAY 85: 2 Kings 24 - 1 Chronicles 2

Living On An Allowance

And as for his provisions, there was a regular ration given him by the king, a portion for each day, all the days of his life.

Five hundred years of disobedience finally reaped a harvest, and the people of Israel were off to captivity.

Their king was shut up in prison in a foreign land until one day the guards opened the door and called his name.

He cleaned himself up, changed his clothes, and followed some strangers into the court of the king of Babylon. He sat down at his assigned seat after too many days in a cell eating scraps and enjoyed some real food. From that day on, the king of Israel lived on an allowance from the king of Babylon.

But kings aren't supposed to live on allowances.

We are kings and priests to our God, seated in heavenly places with him, but the lies we believe about ourselves keep us living within unnecessary limitations.

Like the guy who took his one talent and buried it, our fear manipulates us to "be faithful" and "manage" what we have with the goal of not wasting any of it, but Jesus called that guy wicked and lazy.

You are a KING, the business partner of God, and anything He trusts you with He expects you to double.

Stop living as a vassal of the enemy living on a fixed allowance! We are co-rulers with God, trusted stewards, and creative sons and daughters who take what we have and make more.

DAY 86: 1 Chronicles 3 - 6

The Prayer Of Jabez

Oh, that You would bless me indeed, and enlarge my territory, that Your hand would be with me, and that You would keep me from evil, that I may not cause pain!

Jabez was more honorable than his brothers.

What do you think it means when the Bible says he was more honorable?

When Jabez was born it hurt his mother enough for her to name him "HE WILL CAUSE PAIN."

Imagine walking around as a boy with all your brothers calling you that.

Deep inside him something cried out, "I don't want to be the guy who hurts others!"

So Jabez changed.

He longed to be a blessing to others, to add value instead of taking it away, and it caused him to pray this prayer:

"Oh, that You would bless me indeed, and enlarge my territory, that Your hand would be with me, and that You would keep me from evil, that I may not cause pain!"

Being honorable means that you refuse to accept the status quo, long to add value to others, and WANT MORE so you can be a blessing.

DAY 87: 1 Chronicles 7 - 10

Day & Night

These are the singers, heads of the fathers' houses of the Levites, who lodged in the chambers, and were free from other duties; for they were employed in that work day and night.

On earth as it is in heaven is more than an idea; it's a mandate.

We are called to reproduce the atmosphere of heaven in our heart, home, church, and sphere of influence.

When David was young, out there on the rolling hills worshiping, he got a glimpse of what heaven was like, and he fell in love with God's Presence.

It was his quest to host God's presence as no one had ever done before. He brought back the ark to Jerusalem, built a tent for it, hired full-time musicians and singers to worship around the clock, and frequented the tabernacle himself. For the first time in history, someone had made the Presence top priority, and it paid off in a big way.

We too are called to make His Presence out first priority, and the key to doing that is awareness.

Worship, singing, creative expressions, gratefulness, thanksgiving, music, meditation, prayer, and honor keep us aware of the God we serve and the massive difference His presence makes.

Awareness takes the things that are technically ours in heaven and makes them available to use here on the earth, changing everything. Day and night adoration establishes and maintains our connection with the Holy Spirit, and if we make it priority number one, we will see heaven invade earth.

DAY 88: 1 Chronicles 11 - 14

Holding Your Ground

But they stationed themselves in the middle of that field, defended it, and killed the Philistines. So the LORD brought about a great victory.

Retreating with the others, Eleazar hustled through the field, glancing over his soldier to gauge the advance of the enemy. In the distance, a Philistine warrior raised his spear and thrust it into the back of a man as he ran for his life. Eleazar slowed to a walk, the fire starting to burn within. He knew that man. From the way he ran and the shield he carried, Eleazar could tell that it was a friend he had met the previous week as they prepared for battle. As he crossed the mid-point of the field, Eleazar stopped and turned around. Silently he waited until he identified the enemy soldier who had speared his friend in the back like a coward. As the Philistine came into view, Eleazar positioned himself in his path.

With a cry that drowned out the noise of the battle, he struck the enemy soldier down with one blow of his sword. Emboldened and resolved, Eleazar adjusted for a fight; there is no way I'm giving up another inch of ground he thought. One by one, he began to cut down the enemy as they approached. Many of his people continue to flee, but a few of his brothers stopped and formed ranks amid the barley. They fought into the afternoon without a break. Not one Philistine got through the line they formed, and their courage grew with every passing hour.

Finally, it was over. The stalks of barley were matted and red with blood by the bodies of the enemy that lay all around. Exhausted, Eleazar looked into the eyes of the men who had stood with him. The story spread as if carried by the wind, and soon the legend of that day had brought courage to an entire nation. As men and women throughout the countryside tended to their fields, they thought, "There's no way we're giving up this ground we have worked so hard to cultivate."

DAY 89: 1 Chronicles 15 - 18

The Artist

Then David spoke to the leaders of the Levites to appoint their brethren to be the singers accompanied by instruments of music, stringed instruments, harps, and cymbals, by raising the voice with resounding joy.

Traditionally, ministers are those known for their care for others. We place a high value on those who visit the sick, gather children, perform funeral services, lead meetings, and counsel troubled marriages. These are the shepherds, who care for the sheep. They play a vital role in a healthy community and are worthy of the highest respect.

It should go without saying that loving God with all our heart is priority number one, and loving others as we love ourselves is a close second. Kindness, love, people skills, communication, and community are all irreplaceable components of every Christian life.

But I want to address a less appreciated group of people, the artists. The ones who place a high value on creativity and craftsmanship, who always have a project they are working on-- they are as important as the shepherds.

Throughout the Scriptures, the Spirit of God anointed as many artists as pastors, and their roles were vital to the growth of God's kingdom.

So here's to the creatives: the prophets who live to deliver a MESSAGE, the singers who fashion a SONG, and the authors who give birth to WORDS. The musicians who compose a SOUND, the artists who craft a MASTERPIECE, the craftsman who creates BEAUTY, the technician who designs POSSIBILITIES, and the speaker who offers INSPIRATION, keep up the good work.

DAY 90: 1 Chronicles 19 - 22

A Man Of Rest

Behold, a son shall be born to you, who shall be a man of rest.

You are the Temple of the Holy Spirit, and together we are a House for God. David said, "the house to be built for the LORD must be exceedingly magnificent, famous and glorious throughout all countries."

Not only are you a living stone in the wall of the House of God, but you are also called to build it by equipping and encouraging other people. **Before you can do any productive work, you must become a person of rest.**

Do not get me wrong, there is plenty of work to be done, and tremendous effort is required to build something exceedingly magnificent. Kingdom work, the building up of other people and helping them find their place, requires the power of the Holy Spirit, and the Dove only rests on those who are at rest.

God adopted you as Sons and Daughters; you are forgiven, set free, accepted, and loved. The Father calls you by a new name, giving you a unique identity, and the Spirit comes and dwells in your spirit. All of that is free.

Jesus calls it being born again because it closely resembles being born into a family. From the first moment you enter the world, you are loved, named, accepted, and protected.

However, Satan is an orphan and will tempt you to think like him. If he can get you to work for your acceptance or try and prove your worth, he knows you will never build anything. Once you stop playing Satan' game and learn to rest, you will be able to do significant work in the power of the Spirit.

DAY 91: 1 Chronicles 23 - 26

Prophesying On Harps

Moreover David and the captains of the army separated for the service some of the sons of Asaph, of Heman, and of Jeduthun, who should prophesy with harps, stringed instruments, and cymbals.

David created musical instruments, commissioned people to learn to play them, and paid their salaries to worship full-time.

David wanted them to do more than play-- **he wanted them to prophesy with their instruments.**

The word prophesy means to do something under the influence of the Holy Spirit.

The implication is that speaking is the same as playing an instrument-- you can prophesy doing both.

I have seen this in action with music, but I think it applies to anything.

Can you lead under the influence?

How about parent, teach, write, do customer service, or sell a product?

We have examples of craftsmen, soldiers, and poets under the influence; I wonder what else is possible?

What would it look like if you mastered your craft and lived with enough margin to prophesy with your work?

Be careful though-- **the kingdom may come in your cubicle.**

DAY 92: 1 Chronicles 27 - 2 Chronicles 1

In Writing

"All this," said David, "the LORD made me understand in writing, by His hand upon me, all the works of these plans."

If I have learned anything this year it is this: nothing brings clarity like writing down what God is saying to you.

David discovered this early, writing thousands of words in songs, Psalms, and sayings. But here's the cool part-- he got the plans for the temple, the heavenly pattern of worship, and the wisdom of how to implement it from the Spirit while he wrote!

One thing David penned jumped off the page at me. He said, "I set my affection on the house of God."

Nothing gets stuff done like FOCUSED AMBITION.

David DESIRED to build the temple, not God, but once David FOCUSED his DESIRE firmly one that one thing, **the Lord showed him how to do it.**

He fell in love with God's presence, lived in the place of worship, and longed to build a magnificent house to host the Glory of God.

When you set your affection on something, your attention follows, motivation grows, and God gets excited.

God LOVES to show you HOW to accomplish the ONE BIG THING that your heart desires, and He will reveal it to you in great detail as you write it down.

DAY 93: 2 Chronicles 2 - 5

Mastering Your Craft

And now I have sent a skillful man, endowed with understanding, Huram my master craftsman.

Tyre was an island city off the coast of Lebanon in the Mediterranean Sea known for its shipbuilding, trade, and craftsmanship.

Through their seafaring, they had access to rare materials from around the world, and the hills of Lebanon grew the best timber.

It's no wonder Solomon chose to trade the produce Israel had an abundance of for the building materials needed for the Temple. But what is fascinating is the master craftsman, Huram, that Solomon asked for along with the supplies.

I love the description the king of Tyre gave of Huram, calling him the kind of person who can accomplish any plan you give him.

We are no longer constructing a temple to host God's presence, but **we all have a group of people we are to build up and a set of skills to develop**.

It is not separate from your life's work-- it is your life's work.

Your work matters. Your influence matters. Your skills matter.

Master your craft, and use it to build up the people around you. Create the most beautiful, exciting, and meaningful places and projects, and gather the lonely into families.

We need you at your best.

DAY 94: 2 Chronicles 6 - 9

Healing The Land

If My people who are called by My name will humble themselves, and pray and seek My face, and turn from their wicked ways, then I will hear from heaven, and will forgive their sin and heal their land.

Two thousand years ago Jesus established His kingdom, connecting us to heaven through the Holy Spirit and leaving us with a mission: explore the possibilities of heaven by revelation and make it into reality on earth by faith.

If we pray the prayer but sit down and wait for rescue from the place we are supposed to be transforming, guess what happens? Our cities, regions, and nations don't experience change. "Your will be done, on earth as it is in heaven," we mutter and then say to our friends, "God will judge those people and that place."

If there were tears in heaven, I think the Father might shed one when He sees His people whom He commissioned to disciple nations and make the earth look like heaven sitting on the sidelines hoping it all burns to the ground.

We are called to be fathers and mothers who own the land and adopt the people, who exercise our faith to bless them and leave the area better than we found it.

The promise of God to Solomon still stands, "if My people who are called by My name will humble themselves, and pray and seek My face, and turn from their wicked ways, then I will hear from heaven, and will forgive their sin and heal their land." But as long as it's not our problem, nothing will change. If it is not our people, our sin, and our land, then we will never pray in humble faith for God to heal it.

DAY 95: 2 Chronicles 10 - 13

Who Are You Listening To?

But he rejected the advice which the elders had given him, and consulted the young men who had grown up with him.

One hundred percent of people who live fulfilled and successful lives who have a coach to help them and most high achievers have more than one.

The idea of the independent cowboy riding off into the sunset happy and fulfilled is a myth-- no one becomes successful alone.

You need trusted advisers.

A spouse, friend, or teammate is fine for emotional support, but they're usually in the same stage of life that you are.

You need a pastor, teacher, mentor, or boss who has more experience than you to explain how things work.

Great ministries, marriages, businesses, careers, and organizations develop with time-tested wisdom from those who have been there and done that.

Don't make the blunder that Rehoboam made when he listened to the advice of his young friends instead of his father's trusted counselors.

Finding wise counsel is easier than it’s ever been.

Seek out those who have the results you want and pay close attention to what they have to say.

DAY 96: 2 Chronicles 14 - 17

Looking For Loyalty

For the eyes of the LORD run to and fro throughout the whole earth, to show Himself strong on behalf of those whose heart is loyal to Him.

God is the God of more than enough; there is no limit to His care, provision, or might.

Time does not restrict His awareness, nor urgency demand His attention.

Need cannot outweigh His power, nor opposition challenge His strength.

Death has dominion no longer, and life flows from His being.

Bring your disappointment to Him, and He will help.

Cry out to Him when you feel attacked, and He will defend.

Enter into His presence with a grateful heart, and He will bless.

Set your heart of faith before Him, and He will reward.

Drag your broken heart to Him, and He will heal.

Share your dreams with Him, and He will cheer.

But whatever you do, or however you feel, **don't stay away from Him.** The size of your need means nothing to Him, and the grandness of your dream does not intimidate Him. **It is only the breadth of your loyalty that God is measuring, and He will show Himself strong on behalf of those whose hearts are loyal to Him.**

DAY 97: 2 Chronicles 18 - 21

Chain Of Command

Do not be afraid nor dismayed because of this great multitude, for the battle is not yours, but God's.

Any three-year-old could do it. Talk to God with expectation, listen to what He says, then sing about how great He is. It's so simple that we sometimes neglect to do it, believing there is a more complicated answer to our problem.

What is it about such an elementary process that sets us up to win?

Jesus is the KING of a vast kingdom, and under His command is innumerable angels who work with you and the Holy Spirit to establish His dominion on the earth.

You are an ambassador of that kingdom, a representative of the King in your sphere of influence. When you pray, listen, obey, and praise, it keeps you in alignment with the will of the King. As long as you are talking to Him, following orders, and praising Him in the press, your problems are God's problems.

As an ambassador, you have the authority of the government you represent, and if you are in trouble, the entire military is there to back you up.

Your authority comes from your agreement, and you demonstrate that with your mouth.

Stay in alignment, remain LOYAL, and know your place in the chain of command. As you use your voice to proclaim your allegiance, ask for help, and sing praises, an army of angels, the body of Christ, and the Spirit of God are on call to help fight your battles.

DAY 98: 2 Chronicles 22 - 25

It's Not Worth It

God has power to help and to overthrow.

We have all done it. You make your plans, set things in order, and get ready to act. You may even spend some money getting it all together.

And then, right before you are about to do what you had planned, you feel a check in your spirit. You talk to the Lord about it, and he warns you not to go through with the arrangement.

Amaziah did the same thing. He got the men of Judah together and organized them for battle; then he paid one hundred talents of silver ($100 million) to hire an extra hundred thousand soldiers from Israel.

A man of God shows up and says that if you go to war with those guys, you're never coming back.

"What about my $100 million investment? I won't be able to recoup any of that," Amaziah asked. The man of God responded, "$100 million? God can give you much more than that!"

You see, when God warns you, there is a reason. He is not malicious or stingy; He has your best interest at heart. No matter how far you get down the road of your plan, if God says to put the brakes on, I'd put the brakes on. You can't always anticipate what is around the bend.

Even if you stand to lose $100 million, is it worth your life? I love the man of God's answer when the king asked about the money. **What is a 100 talents of silver to God? He can give you so much more than that if you're listening and loyal.**

DAY 99: 2 Chronicles 26 - 29

Moving Fast

Then Hezekiah and all the people rejoiced that God had prepared the people, since the events took place so suddenly.

Hezekiah began His leadership role at twenty-five years old, and within the first month of taking over after his father died, he was running full speed ahead.

He commissioned the Priests and Levites to consecrate themselves and the House of God, and in just over two weeks, they finished the job.

The king gathered the leaders of the city, told them to bring animals for a burnt offering, and dusted off David's musical instruments.

Immediately they had an all-out revival, sacrificing to the Lord and worshiping with music and singing until they completed all of the burnt offerings.

When it was over, they burst into a celebration because God had prepared the people, since the whole process had only taken a couple of weeks.

Their heads were spinning with the progress made in such a short time.

For a move of God to happen fast, there must be a strong leader who will do anything to see it through, and a group of people prepared to act.

Is there something you have been waiting on for a long time?

May the Lord prepare your heart so things can move quickly in the coming season of your life.

DAY 100: 2 Chronicles 30 - 33

What Are You Made Of?

God withdrew from him, in order to test him, that He might know all that was in his heart.

No grace, prophetic words, anointing, wise counsel, sense of God's presence, or help. Just you, all by yourself.

It's the last minute of the game, you have the ball, and there is nothing anyone can do to help. **It's time to see what you're made of.** Isolated one on one with the enemy, do you have what it takes?

God wouldn't do something like that to you, would He? He did it to Hezekiah, Jesus, and Peter.

There will come a time when you don't feel anything-- no motivation, grace, Presence, correction, direction, or accountability-- what will you do at that moment?

You will act based on how you think about yourself.

Five years from now, the Father will be the same, the Bible will still be true, and Jesus will remain the leader of the church. The Holy Spirit will be encouraging you with similar words as He is right now.

The government and economy won't have changed much. Your negative friends and family will say about the same stuff. Wages, interest, and taxes will be about the same. Problems in society will be pretty close to what they are now.

The difference will come from you, as Jim Rhon says, "If you will change, everything will change for you."

DAY 101: 2 Chronicles 34 - Ezra 1

The Words

Thus says the LORD God of Israel: "Concerning the words which you have heard…"

Through the mouth of prophets, God spoke to every king of Israel-- some heard and obeyed, and others hardened their hearts.

Josiah's tenderness to God's words was noteworthy, and God was impressed.

What we do with THE WORDS that God's speaks to us is the most important thing in our lives.

Jesus' name, according to his friend John, is the WORD of God; He speaks all of the time. The Father's primary role is to name us, reminding us of our purpose and identity. The Holy Spirit is continually giving revelation to all who are paying attention.

Living in the Kingdom of God is entirely about THE WORDS, and our response to them. When the Father reveals your identity, purpose, and worth, what is your response? Intentionally cultivating confidence is the only appropriate action.

When the Son declares the GOOD NEWS to you, what do you do? You take your brokenness to him and refuse to settle for anything less than happiness. When the Spirit whispers ideas that will change your life and those around you, how do you act? Raising your ambition and focusing until you bear fruit is all that you can do.

Living as a believer means developing a tender heart that receives God's WORDS and bears fruit.

DAY 102: Ezra 2 - 5

Mixed Feelings

Old men who had seen the first temple wept with a loud voice when the foundation of this temple was laid before their eyes. Yet many shouted aloud for joy.

Have you ever felt excited about the possibilities ahead, but you also feel down because it is still early in the process, and there's a heap of work left to do?

You don't know if you want to laugh or cry.

Perhaps you remember the good old days when things were more comfortable, or you're comparing your situation to another that seems so much better.

If you are building anything, I'm sure you have experienced these mixed feelings. It is common to feel both excitement and sorrow when you are in the middle of a project.

So what do we do?

Fall in love with the work.

It's in the craftsmanship we find joy. The simple acts of chiseling the stone, shaping the wood, and planning the next step are the fun part.

Destinations never satisfy as much as we imagine-- it's the work that fulfills.

Build relationships, perfect your skills, and set big goals, but stay away from comparison.

You must enjoy the process to finish the work God called you to do.

DAY 103: Ezra 6 - 9

Prospering Through Prophecy

So the elders of the Jews built, and they prospered through the prophesying of Haggai the prophet and Zechariah the son of Iddo.

God speaks to us two types of words: IDENTITY WORDS and IDEA WORDS. Identity words are the loud ones that define who we are. They are often accompanied by impartation, which is the power you will need to become who God said you are. These prophecies are rare and memorable, and they determine the size and type of field your heart will be, and they will always be followed by testing to see if you believe them.

The appropriate response to IDENTITY WORDS is to accept them as gifts from the Father, believe them, and take responsibility to develop your confidence, emotional wholeness, and focused ambition so you can walk them out.

Once your heart is good soil (you believe what God says about you), you are ready to bear fruit. Fruit is the product of your life, and it grows from the seeds (ideas) the Holy Spirit gives you.

Idea words are not loud. They come every day and are usually subtle whispers. Every idea from God begins with the potential to grow into a fruitful plant-- all they need is a good heart to receive them.

When we say things like "The devil must be after me" or "I'm just waiting on God" or "I'm so busy and distracted; my circumstances won't allow me to prosper" we sabotage our fruitfulness.

Quit making excuses and take a step today towards becoming a confident, happy, and focused field that God's words can grow in, and watch as your life begins to prosper.

DAY 104: Ezra 10 - Nehemiah 3

What's In Your Heart?

Then I arose in the night, I and a few men with me; I told no one what my God had put in my heart to do at Jerusalem.

The donkey picked it's way through the rubble, placing each step with care.

The hills were tricky to navigate at night, but the moon was out, so they advanced around the city, assessing the damage.

Decades these stones had laid here-- scorch marks still visible on some. As he slid off to pass under a low gate, Nehemiah pondered the future.

He was not afraid. Months of preparation gave him time to deal with the anxiety, and now he felt cautiously optimistic.

Nehemiah wasn't sure why he circled Jerusalem in the middle of the night. He was announcing his intentions to the world the next day, and a thorough investigation seemed appropriate.

All he knew for sure was **God burned into his heart a passion for rebuilding the city,** and the king showed him unusual favor to help make it happen.

It was now or never.

The morning light peeked over the hill behind him as he rode back into the broken city. He gathered the people and stood atop one of the fallen stones.

"Come and let us build the wall of Jerusalem," Nehemiah announced.

"Let us rise up and build," was their reply.

DAY 105: Nehemiah 4 - 7

Such A Man As I

And I said, "Should such a man as I flee? And who is there such as I who would go into the temple to save his life? I will not go in!"

Dear enemy,

There's no way I'm backing off-- NO WAY. I'm not the kind of guy who runs scared. So make your threats, fake your prophetic words, and try to tempt me, but it's no use. I'm doing a great work for God, so I can't bother listening to your nonsense right now.

I have nothing to prove to you. God put it in my heart to rebuild this city, and the king gave me permission and resources. You have no authority over me, so your threats mean nothing.

Time is of the essence. **My work matters, my heart matters, my people matter. You, well, you don't matter.**

Threaten us, and we will build and fight at the same time. Tempt us, and we will ignore you. Attempt to distract us, and we will worship in your face. We will not stop until we build this wall and restore this city.

I'm the kind of person that hears from God, rebuilds cities, sacrifices for a cause, and leads my people to safety and prosperity.

I will not blame my circumstances for a half-finished project. I will not use the enemy as an excuse to hide. I will not say that I am waiting on God when I should be working.

Such a man as I was born for such a time as this, and I am not missing my opportunity to do something great for God.

DAY 106: Nehemiah 8 - 11

We Will Not Neglect

We will not neglect the house of our God.

Years of being raised by, or neglected by, orphan parents, working dead-end jobs, and fending for yourself creates a protective layer over your heart. You get hard.

The lens you see the world through makes it look cold and distant, and you approach every situation with self-preservation in mind.

Your first thought is to protect yourself because no one has ever looked out for you before.

Arrogance, covered in insecurity, and clothed with false humility, paralyzes any attempt at adding value to others.

Every interaction is a test to ascertain the answer to the only question on their mind: **do you like me now?**

Orphan thinking is no way to build a church, or anything, for that matter.

It is a far cry from the Ephesians 4 model, where anointed leaders equip the body and every believer builds each other up until we look like Christ.

I can tell you from experience; **there is only one answer to an orphan spirit-- repentance.** It is a black hole that no one else can fill.

It is time to stop neglecting the House of our God.

Will you repent for your orphan thinking, renew your mind, and begin building up the people in your community?

DAY 107: Nehemiah 12 - Esther 2

Preparation

Thus were the days of their preparation apportioned: six months with oil of myrrh, and six months with perfumes and preparations for beautifying women.

You're already one of the most beautiful women in the world, and then you're given an entire year to become more attractive. Seems a bit excessive, right? **Not if you're a queen.**

In Ephesians 5, Paul tells us that Christ is the husband and we are His bride. He prepares us with extreme care so we can become radiant and without blemish.

Often, we resist the preparation process because we don't think of ourselves as royalty, but we are the best of the best, chosen by God, covered in light, the treasure of Jesus' heart. You are moving from glory to glory, so here are a few tips from Esther to help you along the way.

Accept your awesomeness. God chose you, gave you an incredible identity, and set you up to succeed. Just roll with it.

Play to your strengths. Comparing yourself is the trap of fools, so avoid it at all cost.

Take all the help you can get. Don't resist the preparation, as if by accepting it you are admitting you are not beautiful already. If you are getting the treatment, that means you are already one of the best.

Trust your coach. God will assign a coach or two to help with the process-- trust them and listen to what they say.

Be brave. God is preparing you for action, so be courageous and go all in.

DAY 108: Esther 3 - 6

While You Are Sleeping

That night the king could not sleep. So one was commanded to bring the book of the records of the chronicles; and they were read before the king.

The fruitful life is a partnership between you and God. The farmer prepares the soil and plants the seed, and God makes it grow.

The wise farmer, who desires to reap all year long, diversifies both the type of seeds she plants and the timing. Instead of planting corn all at once, plant a row every ten days and then add beans alongside it.

Don't plant one fruit, plant many. Strawberries for the spring, then cherries, blackberries, and finally apples in the fall. Set out your garlic while you are still picking kale and broccoli, and you will have it ready to eat when it gets warm again.

Build a greenhouse, then add a freezer and some canning jars, and you're all set. **Here's the point-- next January you're going to want some strawberry jam on your biscuit, and you can have it if you prepare.**

When Mordecai was alerting the officials about two guys plotting to kill the king, he did not know that he would need a favor down the road, it was just the right thing to do. But while he was sleeping one night, God kept the king awake and used what had been sown a long time ago to bring the deliverance he needed.

Diversify your prayers, giving, kindness, content creation, acts of service, and identity.

Then one night while you are sleeping, the thing that you planted months ago will bear fruit, and you will be so glad you prepared ahead of time.

DAY 109: Esther 7 - 10

Second Chair

For Mordecai the Jew was second to King Ahasuerus, and was great among the Jews and well received by the multitude of his brethren, seeking the good of his people and speaking peace to all his countrymen.

Joseph, Daniel, and Mordecai are among the legends of leadership in the Bible, but they were never in charge.

We admire the likes of David, Solomon, and Jesus, who were the front men for great movements, and we should. It takes tremendous effort, skill, anointing, and commitment to be the face of an organization. But behind the spokesperson, there's always the guys and girls who get stuff done.

Scripture says Mordecai was great, well received, sought the good of his people, and spoke peace to them-- and he did it all from the second chair, influencing the king on behalf of God's agenda.

Behind the scenes leaders are usually prophetic, giving understanding to the king. Wise counsel, insight into the future, and prophetic direction are incredibly valuable to anyone in charge-- as long as it comes with a loyal heart.

Most leaders never sit atop their organizations, but that does not diminish their importance.

Wherever you rank in the organizational chart of your family, job, business, ministry, organization, or church, follow Mordecai's example. Seek the good of people and speak peace to them, giving excellent advice and support to those above and below you.

Making other people successful makes you fruitful.

DAY 110: Job 1 - 4

The Answer

While he was still speaking, another also came and said...

In the middle of a couple of hundred years of blessing, Job had one awful year. Everything that could go wrong went wrong, and there was no apparent reason.

Questions were everywhere. God was asking Satan questions, Satan was asking God questions, Job inquired, his wife demanded, and his friends challenged.

What is going on? Why did this happen? Whose fault is it? How do I stop the pain? What did I do wrong?

But there were no answers.

The entire book of Job is one big question: "Where is the person who could mediate between God and man, between the spiritual and the natural?"

Jesus is the answer. He revealed the Father, took care of sin and death, restored human dignity, and got our authority back from Satan.

He said, "In this world, you will have trouble, but be of good cheer, I have overcome the world."

Now I have control of my heart. I have a comforter, an advocate, who fights for me. I can repent and think like God, and see from His perspective. When a test comes, I have all the grace I need to get through it with flying colors. Fear, anger, doubt, and shame have no place in my life.

Finally, I have what matters most-- I have a relationship with God.

DAY 111: Job 5 - 8

Honesty vs. Truth

Therefore I will not restrain my mouth; I will speak in the anguish of my spirit; I will complain in the bitterness of my soul.

HAPPY is normal, and PEACE is our standard of living. Therefore, when we talk, our speech should reflect the faith in our hearts, our hope for a bright future, and the love we feel for others.

However, to stay happy in a world where things don't always work out the way we hope, we must take an honest look at our hearts.

Truth has no feelings; it is absolute. God is good, Satan is bad, and Jesus died for your sins. Those are irrefutable truths that will never change, no matter how you feel. But as you stand under the protection of those truths, like an umbrella in the rain, you must be honest.

Sometimes things hurt deep, and the last thing you need is to pretend. Your feelings will never change the truth of who God is, but they still matter, and for them to get healed, you must talk about them.

We never have permission to hurt others or stay bitter, nor do we dump our garbage on people who cannot help. Instead, take your honest feelings to Jesus, without blame or shame, and stay there and talk to Him until He heals the wound in your heart. Then find a trusted friend, pastor, spouse, or mentor, and tell them what is going on inside.

Take full responsibility for the things you did wrong, whether accidental or on purpose., but do not pretend. Jesus can heal anything, given an honest heart to work with, but if we pretend it creates a divide inside of us that will result in unmanageable stress. Take your real feelings to Him, say what you need to say, and let Him fix it.

DAY 112: Job 9 - 12

Weep With Those Who Weep

Should your empty talk make men hold their peace?

People say weird things during a crisis.

After losing a baby through miscarriage, we were "comforted" by people offering their opinions:

"God must think you are so strong to let you go through something like this."

"The devil must be after you because he knows you are a threat to him."

"You can always try again and have another baby."

SERIOUSLY?

Do you think your opinion about doctrine is what my broken heart needs?

When someone has a broken heart, they don't need your help to assign blame; they need a hug.

I found out there are only two things that help during a loss: **the voice of God and comfort from someone who knows how you feel.**

So, if you have a word from God, share it in love.

If you genuinely know how someone feels, be there for them.

But if you do not have either one of those, please, hug them and listen with care, and keep your opinions to yourself.

DAY 113: Job 13 - 16

Living With Margin

But I would strengthen you with my mouth, And the comfort of my lips would relieve your grief.

Imagine a wild and beautiful place, untouched by human hands for decades. Huge trees shade untamed streams, and predators stalk their prey in the shadows. I've been to a few places like that. I've seen wild otters playing in crystal rivers, and bald eagles chasing screeching wood ducks.

Trees grow tall in such places, but they also collapse in the storm, get destroyed by pests, and burn in wildfires. Berries blossom along sunny paths, but they're usually small and the birds and bears share them.

The natural tendency of untended things is survival. Grape vines grow long, searching for the sun, and spread out with many leaves, but there is little energy left for the grapes. **Left alone, we don't bear fruit.**

Now imagine a well cared for orchard or garden. Every plant is placed in the optimal place in the sun, watered on purpose, fertilized, protected from pests, and pruned. Nothing is left to chance; everything is intentional.

Fruitfulness comes from living with a margin, where we have time, energy, revelation, and power to spare. It is the opposite of survival.

Let God prune you-- focus on a few things and operate at 80% capacity. Leave 20% of your energy, time, money, revelation, and anointing to produce creative solutions for other people's problems.

Develop a rhythm of rest, worship, personal growth, and relationships that recharges your batteries. Live self-aware. Learn how to get back to happiness when you start to drift, and soon fruit will grow in your life.

DAY 114: Job 17 - 20

The Anchor

For I know that my Redeemer lives, And He shall stand at last on the earth.

There are times in everyone's life when nothing feels stable. Circumstances are swirling around, the ground is moving under our feet, and we're holding on for dear life.

Death, divorce, or disease grab us by the throat and shake us, and everything movable gets moved.

Job was in one of those seasons.

Nothing made sense.

His life was tossed about by the wind and waves of adversity, and nothing was reliable-- except one thing.

"For I know that my Redeemer lives, and He shall stand at last on the earth; and after my skin is destroyed, this I know, that in my flesh I shall see God, whom I shall see for myself, and my eyes shall behold, and not another. How my heart yearns within me!"

There is one thing completely reliable, an anchor in the storm-- **Jesus rose from the dead, and He lives to make intercession for you.**

Live or die, you will live forever with your God.

You can count on it, and build your hopes on it; He is the ROCK you can trust with your future. If everything else fails, one thing will remain, your Redeemer lives, and you will see Him for yourself.

DAY 115: Job 21 - 24

Why?

Oh, that I knew where I might find Him, That I might come to His seat!

Remember being a kid, lost in your little world? You eat, drink, play, sleep, play some more.

The whole planet revolves around you, as far as you know.

All is grand until something happens that you don't understand. Someone tells you no, or makes you mad, or forces you to clean up your mess. A friend is mean to you, or a loved one gets sick, and **you want to know WHY?**

What you yearn for, but do not know how to express, is to know that everything is alright, that someone cares about you. An answer to your questions would not satisfy because you wouldn't understand the answers anyway. You need a hug.

So it is with God and us. Sometimes we drag our feet, refusing to give any effort until He answers the WHY in our hearts, but we are only hurting ourselves.

Like the 4-year-old, our hearts yearn for reassurance that God is looking out for us, that we are safe, loved, accepted.

Stop connecting your trust and effort to having answers to all your questions. Be willing to live with a little mystery, and remember how God has consistently been there for you.

Lean into His presence, see His smile, and feel His embrace. Everything is going to be OK.

DAY 116: Job 25 - 28

The Price Of Wisdom

And to man He said, 'Behold, the fear of the Lord, that is wisdom, And to depart from evil is understanding.'

There is a way things work, and you don't make the rules. If you don't believe me, try this-- go outside and try to keep the sun from going down tonight. You can try, but your success rate will hover around 0%.

THE CREATOR makes the rules.

Jesus is the only way to the Father, the only sacrifice for sin-- you either fall on that rock, or it falls on you. It does not matter if you like it or not, it's just the way things are.

He leads, you follow. That is the cost of doing business with God.

If you do not like it, you can try to launch out on your own and do things however you want, but that is going to end poorly for you.

Wisdom is seeing from God's perspective, and understanding the way things work so that you can cooperate with Him and get great results, and it is the most valuable thing on the planet.

The price for wisdom is high: honor, respect, submission, patience, and fear. If you attempt to buy it with pride, hurry, or neglect, understanding will laugh you out of the store.

Purchasing wisdom is costly but worth it. When you have it, you have everything-- you have God as your business partner.

Are you willing to pay the price?

DAY 117: Job 29 - 32

The Infinite Game

Oh, that the Almighty would answer me, That my Prosecutor had written a book!

Jesus changed the game two thousand years ago. He beat death, crucified our sin nature, took Satan's authority, and invited us to play a new game.

The new game is not a finite game of victim versus villain, where we either win or lose against sin every day. It is an infinite game, and the object of the game is to keep playing.

We already won. We are seated in heavenly places right now, the cries of holy, holy, holy ringing in our ears. There is no sin nature to play with; it's dead.

The point of the new game is discovery and wonder, relationship and pleasure. **It's like like romping through the woods with your dad, seeing what you can see.** There is no scoreboard, innings, or umpires.

As we set our minds on things above, life is so much more fun. The endless revelation leads to daily growth, and we fall in love with the work.

Like being in a research and development lab stocked with every kind of possibility, we enjoy the daily process of discovery, working with God to invent solutions.

Together with our Father, we play each day not to win or lose, but to keep the game going. We take pleasure in His company, and we look forward to the progress we will make together. So sorry, old nature, you're on your own. I'm not going to resurrect you every day to play that age-old finite game you like so much. I've got better things to do.

DAY 118: Job 33 - 36

Avoiding Judgment

Let us choose to us judgment: let us know among ourselves what is good.

Judgment is a small person's game.

Little people look up at those above and assume they know why another acted a certain way.

On and on they ramble, searching for fitting words to criticize and condemn while they sit on the couch, unwilling to lift a finger to help.

Judgment requires nothing of you.

The opposite of judgment is compassion.

Compassion requires that you understand your identity, stay whole emotionally, and focus your ambition.

Compassion demands that you lead.

Judgment is for victims and beggars, who assume and blame their way to average.

Compassion is for Kings and Queens, who become the kind of people who change things.

Which will you be?

"For God did not send His Son into the world to condemn the world, but that the world through Him might be saved."

DAY 119: Job 37 - 40

Prepare Yourself Like A Man

Now prepare yourself like a man; I will question you, and you shall answer Me.

There is a terrifying beauty in the whirlwind.

God speaks. Endless activity swirls around, but inside is perfectly calm.

Everything in you screams to run for your life, but you can't move-- it's mesmerizing.

Fear grips you as the Creator's voice thunders, **"Now prepare yourself like a man."**

On shaky legs, you stand to your feet, like a blade of grass trying to stay upright in the wind.

Question after question rumbles at you, but you have no answers.

There is just no way to describe how small you feel.

Revelation overwhelms your senses. You realize that you can't make one drop of water, not one snowflake, regardless of how hard you try.

There are billions of stars, animals, people, organisms-- and a lifetime of learning leaves you with 1% of 1% of the knowledge available.

Holy... holy... holy... is all you can say. Somehow you are relieved, happy, terrified, and amazed at the same.

The Creator knows your name and loves you-- remarkable.

DAY 120: Job 41 - Psalm 2

I Prosper In Everything

His delight is in the law of the LORD.

Can one habit change everything in your life? Here is the promise: if you delight yourself in the words of God, what He has said and is saying, every area of your life will prosper.

If this is true, and I believe it to be so, it is the most remarkable promise ever made. It seems like more people would give it a try, considering the potential benefits.

I'm going to put this promise to the test and see for myself. So far, to the degree that I have put it into practice, it has worked, and here are a few things I've learned.

The revelation comes as much in the output as in the input. Many of my best ideas come through conversations with friends and writing.
God knows everything about everything. Do not limit His influence on your life to just spiritual things.
Study the Bible many different ways-- listen, read, study, meditate, pray.
Practice journaling. When you hear from God, think it through, pray about it, talk to others about it, and write it down.
God does not speak only to you. If you limit what you know to what you can learn from the Scriptures or God directly, you are missing out. Others have spent years drilling deep wells on particular topics. Search them out and learn all you can from them.
Harness your subconscious. Let ideas simmer in the back of your mind and pay attention to dreams.
Ask questions. If God knows everything and desires for you to prosper, why not ask Him about your current dilemma?

DAY 121: Psalms 3 - 6

Gladness Of Heart

You have put gladness in my heart.

Perfect conditions do not exist-- someone is always getting sick, acting crazy, being stupid, or mad about something-- at least that's how it feels. If you are looking for a reason to be upset, you will find one every day of your life. If you are waiting for ideal circumstances to make you happy, it may take awhile.

David discovered another option, an alternative way to live.

A rival of his had a plentiful harvest, more grain and wine than usual, and it triggered his pride. He started spouting nonsense that drove David crazy. Instead of the typical solutions-- firing back with accusations, grumbling in anger, or taking matters in his own hands-- David turned his heart to the Lord.

He channeled his feelings into prayer, cried out to God, and waited. When God spoke to him, he received it with joy and laid down to rest. Quietly on his bed, David meditated on what the Lord said. **The longer he thought about what God revealed to him, and all of the times God had come through in the past, the happier David got.**

"You have put gladness in my heart, more than in the season their grain and wine increased," David sang with a smile. Turn to God in prayer and worship, waiting for Him to speak to you. When you get an answer, rest in it, meditate on it and allow it to wash away all of your frustration.

The path to gladness of heart travels not through the land of perfect conditions, but along the shore of the perfect love of God.

DAY 122: Psalms 7 - 10

Crowned With Glory

For You have made him a little lower than the angels, And You have crowned him with glory and honor.

God ordained my words to carry weight and silence the enemy.

When I think about the Creator and the vast array of His handiwork, it boggles my mind-- how does He pay attention to me?

He thinks of me often, even comes to visit, and it never ceases to amaze me.

I have a place of authority in His kingdom, and He crowns me with glory and honor.

God gave me dominion over the works of His hands, and all things are under my feet.

The earth is my responsibility to maintain.

What should I do with all of this authority?

Should I act like an orphan or victim?

Should I oppress others and join forces with the enemy?

I will do the job for which God has put me on the planet, shut the mouth of the enemy, take responsibility for the world around me, and build up the people in my life. And I will sing the praises of the Creator, from whom and to who are all things.

DAY 123: Psalms 11 - 14

What Are You Known For?

For the LORD is righteous; he loves righteous deeds; the upright shall behold his face.

He always does the right thing.

Always.

When you think of God, you think of righteousness, justice, mercy, and love.

God talks about justice and follows through with righteous action so much that He has become known for it.

Righteousness is God's brand.

What are you known for?

What do you always talk about, celebrate, reward, and produce?

How would others describe your brand?

Because God is the expert on righteousness, the upright are attracted to Him.

They are the ones who get face time with Him, who get to know His heart.

Consistently love, talk about, sell others on, and do the right thing.

Your reward will be seeing the face of God.

DAY 124: Psalms 15 - 18

Fullness Of Joy

The lines have fallen to me in pleasant places; Yes, I have a good inheritance.

If you think like a son, you get to know the Father.

He is so beautiful-- full of love, kindness, and generosity-- that nothing else matters.

Life is not about the money, fame, impact, or comfort; you live for His smile.

As a son, God himself is your inheritance-- your reward is being in His presence.

The orphan, on the other hand, lives for the stuff.

Orphans feel like God is against them because their insecurity keeps them from knowing the heart of the Father, so they take what they can get while they can get it.

But miss the one thing that satisfies.

There is satisfaction in a job well done, healthy relationships, miracles, and provision.

It is the satisfaction of being like your Father and doing what He would do.

But nothing compares to the fullness of joy, the sheer pleasure, of being with Him, hearing His voice, and feeling His presence.

It's perfect.

DAY 125: Psalms 19 - 22

Praying For Yourself

Let the words of my mouth and the meditation of my heart Be acceptable in Your sight, O LORD, my strength and my Redeemer.

There is only one variable in your story-- just one thing that you control.

God is already good.

Jesus died for you and rose again.

The Holy Spirit empowers and comforts you.

The devil's authority expired when Jesus got up from the grave.

The Bible remains the foundation to build on.

Those things will never change; **the only variable is the way you think about yourself.**

Do you believe everything the Father says about you? Have you taken Jesus up on His offer to heal every wound in your heart? Are you clear about God's destiny for your life, and are you taking focused, faith-filled action towards it?

If your heart and mind are central to a fruitful life, and they are, **why not pray for yourself more?** David did it.

"Oh God, help! Warn me when something unexpected is coming. Cleanse me from victim thinking. Convict me when I act like an orphan. Let my words and thoughts about myself line up perfectly with the way You think about me."

DAY 126: Psalms 23 - 26

He Restores My Soul

The LORD is my shepherd; I shall not want.

I am not alone. I am not weary, nor am I scattered. The Lord is my Lord, and I willingly submit. Control is overrated-- I accept comfort and guidance over control every time.

I shall not want. I rest in abundance and sleep in more than enough. To drink deep and be refreshed is easy for me. **I am set up to succeed.** When life nicks and tears at me, He restores my soul.

My mind is renewed, in perfect agreement with Him. My emotions are whole, in precise alignment with truth. **My will is to do His will.** He always leads me down the right path; I never worry about which way to go.

Shame and fear try to cast a long shadow over me, but they fail miserably; it is hard to be afraid with so much comfort and protection.

You sit me down to feast and make my enemies watch, to rub their faces in my success. The dogs bark animosity in the distance, but Your singing over me drowns them out. I have so much more revelation, provision, love, and wisdom than I can ever use-- it's too much.

You cover my mind with your anointing, empowering me inside and out. My cup runs over. I am so blessed that others seek me out, and no matter how much I give, there's always more.

Good things keep happening to me at an alarming rate, and even when I deserve no, you say yes. The Lord's house is now my house, and I can access my King at any time, forever.

DAY 127: Psalms 27 - 30

Free From Fear

In this I will be confident.

Fear is the first step down the road to failure. It causes victim thinking, making you defensive and self-centered, and results in your words agreeing with the enemy. Any faith you had gives way to doubt, and you stop taking risks and trusting the Lord.

Fear invites doubt, shame, blame, isolation, and insecurity into your heart, and pauses everything that God desires to do in your life.

But there is another way-- a way that guarantees confidence in the face of fear.

David said, "In this I will be confident. One thing I have desired of the LORD, That will I seek: That I may dwell in the house of the LORD All the days of my life, To behold the beauty of the LORD, And to inquire in His temple."

Confidence comes from knowing that your favorite place is the secret place.

A loyal heart that seeks the secret place when no one else knows or cares is the antidote for fear.

When you enter into His presence with no agenda except love, shame and blame can't come in with you.

When your will is to do God's will, the enemy can do nothing to hurt you.

You are perfectly safe and confident, and nothing can make you afraid.

DAY 128: Psalms 31 - 34

Aggressive Waiting

But those who seek the LORD shall not lack any good thing.

There is no want to those who fear Him, and those who seek the Lord shall not lack any good thing. What incredible promises! **If these are true, why do we still lack and want?** I believe the answer may lie in something I call aggressive waiting.

Sometimes we misunderstand the sovereignty of God, thinking that He is supposed to live our lives for us, but that is not the case. The Father gives each of us a unique identity and then empowers us to walk it out, but our typical response is to wait on God to make us become who He said we are.

Instead, try these tips so you can "wait" on God the way He intended:

- Take every word from God seriously, as if your life depended on it.
- Use the promises as weapons to fight in prayer until fulfillment.
- Talk to yourself according to the identity God gave you.
- Declare your promises out loud as if one hundred percent accurate.
- Take responsibility to build the confidence you need to walk them out.
- Take your broken heart to Jesus as often as necessary for healing.
- Simplify your life so that you can focus on the things that bear fruit.
- Purposefully turn your small desires into burning ambition.
- Find a coach who is where you want to be to speed up the process.
- Learn the necessary skills you will need to fulfill God's destiny for your life.
- Seek out mutually beneficial relationships in your sphere of influence.

Waiting on God should look like a son or daughter interning for the position God has called them to, not sitting on the couch whining about life.

DAY 129: Psalms 35 - 38

Vindicate Me, O God!

Vindicate me, O LORD my God, according to Your righteousness.

You are doing the right thing, you know it. There's no malice in your heart, your ear is attentive to God's voice, and you're quick to obey. You genuinely love God and people and want to add value to others.

"Why am I facing such opposition?" you wonder. The temptation is to retreat inward, or start complaining, but that never works. False humility tells you that it must be your fault, pride blames it on everyone else, but neither of those feels right. You sowed, watered, weeded, and waited. The crop you planted grew, and then right before harvest time, a hail storm smashed it all. **It's just not fair.**

You could quit, but you know that is not going to end well. You could pull back and give a half-hearted effort in protest. You could whine and complain to everyone you see about how unfair life is. However, those options are all orphan options, spiteful ramblings of a victim spirit.

Thankfully, you bought insurance. All those weeks and months of investing time, money, and effort building a relationship with God is about to pay off. You have what others don't, the Creator as your business partner.

"Vindicate me, O Lord!" you cry out to Him in secret. Passion and confidence swell within you as you plead your case, knowing that on the other end of the line is the most loving, willing, and powerful Being in the universe.

Eventually, He speaks-- He always speaks. His voice is like a warm hug and His words like a discovered treasure, and you know everything will be alright.

DAY 130: Psalms 39 - 42

My Soul Thirsts For God

My soul thirsts for God, for the living God.

I thirst. My mind longs for clarity, but the fog of life surrounds me. My heart yearns for peace, yet stress and anxiety demand my attention. My desire is waning-- I need God.

Days have passed, one after another. Tragedy, moral failure, or disaster has not struck-- only the dull ache and listlessness of dehydration. I caffeinate and compensate, but the temporary lift pushes me away from my destination.

I can feel the life draining from me. I go through the motions, but my energy and enthusiasm are long gone, and my reflexes are slow. The keen mind, deep compassion, and burning desire ordinarily available is now irritation and headache.

I need water. Chewing on a sermon won't do, and it is too late for sipping on a good conversation. Rest cannot help me, or work-- there is only one solution.

Finally, I arrive. I walk into my room and shut the door, locking it behind me. Headphones in my ears, I begin to drink. The Psalms wash over me, like the deep pool under a waterfall pulling me deeper. Worship, intimate and raw, flows from my heart through my lips. I groan and cry, laugh and dance.

He is here, in the room with me. I drink. With no sense of time, I drink, and drink, and drink. My mind begins to clear, peace and joy rise within, and desire starts to burn again. **My soul thirsts for God and nothing else will do.**

DAY 131: Psalms 43 - 46

Confident Kings

Gird Your sword upon Your thigh, O Mighty One, With Your glory and Your majesty.

When you behold Jesus, you become like Him, and He is the King. He died to restore your nobility, to make you a king on the earth. **Your destiny is to rule.** As you renew your mind, restore your heart, and reinvigorate your desires in the presence of Jesus, there are a few things you should expect.

Your physical body, appearance, and personality will become more beautiful and attractive.

You will become an excellent and empowering communicator.

Blessing from God will rest on you.

You will become a brave and mighty warrior fighting for others.

Your life will prosper in every area.

Truth, humility, and righteousness will become your primary values.

You will never stop learning and growing.

Your purpose will align perfectly with God's will.

You will be the happiest person you know.

Your relationships will flourish.

If you want to be like Jesus, you desire to be a king on the earth-- stop resisting nobility and start pursuing it.

DAY 132: Psalms 47 - 50

Sing With Understanding

For God is the King of all the earth; Sing praises with understanding.

He is the great King over all the earth.

We get that part most of the time.

God is big and powerful, the Creator of the ends of the earth.

Armed with that understanding we sing, lifting high the name of our God.

But the greatness of God is only half the revelation we need.

The other side of the story, the part we often overlook, is that **He works through us.**

The Father gathers us into families and chooses an inheritance for us. We receive places, people, ideas, and spheres of influence to govern, and without our cooperation, the job doesn't get done.

The Lord Most High is awesome, without a doubt.

He is the great King over all the earth, for sure.

However, He chooses to rule by giving us an inheritance to be responsible for and subduing the nations under our feet.

With the full understanding of the weight of His glory and ours, we should sing praises-- **we can't appreciate God's greatness without joining the team that is restoring the earth with Him.**

DAY 133: Psalms 51 - 54

Planted In His Presence

I am like a green olive tree in the house of God.

Sure, I have money, but I don't trust it.

My relationships are healthy, but they don't sustain my joy.

The work that I do is meaningful, and I love it, but it's not my source.

My soul prospers, as well as my health, but not because of hobbies, recreation, or friendships.

I flourish in good times and bad because I am rooted and grounded in LOVE.

I am like a green olive tree in the house of God. I blossom and bear fruit, planted in His presence.

Let others boast in their riches, technology, and knowledge while they do evil in their hearts-- it's only a matter of time before they dry up.

But not me.

I have a source that never runs dry, a fountain of living waters.

My confidence is in God's mercy, and I will never be ashamed.

You did this, God.

You earned my trust because of your incredible goodness, and I will sing from the rooftops how reliably kind you are.

DAY 134: Psalms 55 - 58

When I Am Afraid

Whenever I am afraid, I will trust in You.

God is for me. He rewards those who diligently seek Him, so I mine the depths of God to find the treasure He hides for me.

God has proven to me again and again that I can trust Him, but sometimes, even though I know God is reliable, **I get afraid.**

A new challenge arises I have never faced before, people lash out to oppose me, or resistance attempts to pull me down.

I know God is good, and I often seek Him. I should be able to overcome fear with this formula, but it is not always that simple. I need something specific I can hold on to when my emotions go haywire. **I need a word from God.**

When I am afraid I require more than the general knowledge that God is for me, I need specifics. It is time to pull out the prophetic words, testimonies, and scriptures that God has given me, find the ones referring to this aspect of my life, and remember.

In the middle of a fight, when emotions are not my friend, and everything seems backward, intentional remembering is my greatest weapon. But what if I can't remember anything God has said to me about these particular circumstances?

I get alone with God, Bible in hand, and ask. I'm willing to wait, and keep knocking until God opens the door and reveals the truth, then use that word to fight. My emotions may be screaming, and circumstances may look dire, but I refuse to accept anything that does not agree with the WORD.

DAY 135: Psalms 59 - 62

The Fertile Soul

My soul, wait silently for God alone, For my expectation is from Him.

Imagine your soul-- your thoughts, feelings, desires, and decisions-- as an acre of ground. Before God redeemed you, the enemy controlled your heart-- you were waiting on God's help, and you didn't even realize it.

He sent someone to tell you the good news about Jesus, you believed it, and God took your faith in Jesus and used it to cancel your debts and destroy the enemy's hold over you.

The Father's desire is for you to feel a part of the family, understand your unique purpose, voluntarily choose to obey and worship Him, and tend to your heart.

That acre of ground is yours, not God's, and its condition is your responsibility.

Jesus has many ideas for you about the people you will bless, the projects you will build, and the impact you will have, **but those ideas are only as good as the ground in which they grow.**

We cultivate the confidence of a son or daughter of God.

We unearth the stones of fear, anger, shame, blame, and guilt and allow Jesus to heal us.

We cut out the weeds of busyness, compensation, and confusion and focus our ambition on God's will for our lives.

Our fruitfulness is our responsibility.

DAY 136: Psalms 63 - 66

Positive Self Talk

My soul shall be satisfied as with marrow and fatness, and my mouth shall praise You with joyful lips.

How you think about yourself, and what you say to yourself, will determine your future.

Remember Jesus' words in Mark 11-- if you do not doubt in your heart, then you will have whatever you say.

Sounds simple, right? Just believe in your heart without wavering what God has said about you, then say what you want.

No problem.

Sure, it's no problem, until you try it.

First, you must understand your identity by discovering what the Father thinks about you, aligning yourself fully with it, and removing any doubt.

Once you've done that, you use your tongue as the rudder to steer your life towards your destiny.

First, you believe in your heart, then you confess with your mouth-- you must do both.

Consider how David talked to himself in Psalm 63: "My soul shall be satisfied as with marrow and fatness, And my mouth shall praise You with joyful lips."

That's how world changers talk to themselves.

DAY 137: Psalms 67 - 70

He Gives Power To His People

The God of Israel is He who gives strength and power to His people.

What if God could only answer your prayers through you?

Now, hold on, don't start arguing with me yet. This question is not a theology lesson; it is a self-awareness exercise.

God is the One who rides on the heavens, who sends out His mighty voice and changes the course of history. He is awesome. However, throughout the Scripture we see Him answer the prayers of His people through a person. The God of Israel gives strength and power to His people-- His nature is to empower people whenever possible.

So, back to the question. **What if God could only answer your prayers through you?**

What if when you prayed for someone to receive healing, you had to be the only one laying hands on them?

What if your influence was the only means to change your region?

What if demonic oppression only left because of the anointing on your life?

If the only power and strength God could display on the earth were through your life, how would the world look? I think it would look close to the way it does right now.

If we all asked ourselves that question, evaluated ourselves honestly, and took steps to increase our faith, what would the world look like then?

DAY 138: Psalms 71 - 74

Teach Me To Pray

But I will hope continually, And will praise You yet more and more.

For things to change on the earth, a human being must speak the words-- God has delegated that authority to us.

We ask, declare, praise, agree, prophesy, and proclaim, and our words connect heaven and earth through the Holy Spirit living inside of us.

When our words originate in the heart of God, and we believe they matter, things change.

The Spirit begins working inside us, angels are sent to help, people are attracted to assist, power is released, and revelation comes from heaven-- all because we prayed.

I found myself struggling and unsure what to do recently, and God gave me Psalm 71 to pray, and what a gift it has been.

I pray it as written, in the first person, as if I wrote it.

It is effortless to declare with faith because it is word for word Scripture, so I know it agrees with God's will, it came as a word from God to me, so I know it applies to my situation, and it aligns with the desires in my heart so I can pray it with emotion and conviction.

Perhaps God has another prayer for you that is specific to your life-- ask Him and find out.

But if not, use this powerful Psalm as the cry of your heart and watch your life begin to change.

DAY 139: Psalms 75 - 78

Living Happy

I will also meditate on all Your work, And talk of Your deeds.

That sadness you feel, it's not normal-- Jesus made it possible for you to live genuinely happy because there are no cracks in your heart, and here's how you do it.

Become a master at self-awareness, which will allow you to avoid false humility and pride, appreciate the gifts of others, and continually grow.

Properly grieve your losses. If something happens to you that is not fair, you must take the time to cry, grieve, and process what happened.

Admit when you make a mistake. Take responsibility for your heart, mind, and actions, and if you make a mistake, own it.

Always want more than you have. The hungry heart is the happy heart, so always be learning, growing, and expanding your territory.

Forgive. Let go of the debts others owe you as quick as you can.

Fully repent of all sin. Attack anything that even hints at orphan thinking with aggressive repentance and renewal.

Initiate reconciliation with others. Don't wait for them to come to you, go to them and fix what you can that stands between you.

Set boundaries with abusive people. Those who mistreat you for doing the right thing or undervalue you do not get a voice in your life. You can compassionately minister to them, but they do not get to speak into you.

DAY 140: Psalms 79 - 82

Do You Believe Me Now?

"Oh, that My people would listen to Me, That Israel would walk in My ways!"

God has spoken to you; I know He has.

He told you something about who you are and how you can love others well-- He is a Father and He talks to His kids.

The question is, do you believe Him?

If we allow insecurity to have a voice in our hearts, it makes us stubborn.

God tells us who we are over and over again, but we refuse to fully embrace it until we can prove it.

But things don't work that way.

God words contain creative desire and power to bring fulfillment, but you must believe them. The Father's voice defines you, not your insecurity--there is no comparison or proof needed.

When the Father names us, we agree and do the things that our best selves would do.

God said I am a prophet, so I prophesy. God said I am a teacher, so I teach. God said I am a wife, so I find a man and love him better than he loves himself.

Try it. **Ask yourself what you would do if what God said about you was already true, then do those things.**

DAY 141: Psalms 83 - 86

Strength To Strength

Blessed is the man whose strength is in You, Whose heart is set on pilgrimage.

Every day I set my heart on a pilgrimage.

Every day I find strength in my God.

I am a Son; I live with my Father and enjoy His Presence.

I awake in God's house after resting all night in His mercy.

My thirsty soul drinks in His goodness and the cry of my heart is satisfied in His love.

Like a bird leaving the security of its nest, I launch out for the day. I am unafraid-- I will be back soon.

Throughout the day I encounter people and problems, each an opportunity.

Every dry place I cover with living water, and every parched soul drinks from the fountain inside me.

The stronghold of the palace becomes the strength of an ambassador as I represent God in the world. My work is meaningful, adding value to many, but I long to return.

I arrive back home to gifts of grace and glory.

His house is my house, His presence my home.

I lack nothing, nothing at all.

DAY 142: Psalms 87 - 90

Chosen

I have exalted one chosen from the people.

God chose you to bless you and make you a blessing in the earth. You have been handpicked to feel the love of the Father and hear Him call you by name. The joy you experience in His presence is not an accident; God made you that way. **You have been set up to succeed.**

Jesus is about to make every one of your experiences work out for your good. Your mind is calibrated to hear His voice, and your heart is tuned to feel His love. **It's your time.**

God anointed you for a reason-- the world needs you. Every test you face you will pass, and you will walk out of survival in the power of the Spirit. You will know the joy of healthy relationships. The hold of insecurity will break, and you will build the confidence you need to win.

The pain of emotional brokenness is lifting; you are becoming happy and whole. Stress and distractions no longer control your life. Desire is turning into focused ambition, and you will bear much fruit.

Those around you are blessed to know you, and your legacy will impact many generations. The power of the Spirit operates in you, making you MORE THAN ABLE to do the impossible. Your FAITH will not fail, your HOPE will not disappoint, and your LOVE will grow.

Those who oppose you will not outwit you. Wisdom is yours, and revelation. **You are not an accident.** You have a name, a purpose, an identity, a family, an origin, and a bright future.

You are one of the mighty ones who will see heaven invade earth.

DAY 143: Psalms 91 - 94

The Bottleneck

Those who are planted in the house of the LORD Shall flourish in the courts of our God.

Imagine a funnel. You pour stuff through the opening at the top, and at the bottom is an opening through which things flow out. Simple, right?

Your life is like that funnel.

The top is your intimacy with Jesus. You abide in Him, drink from Him, rest in Him, meditate on His words, worship Him, listen to Him, and talk to Him allowing revelation, power, grace, and love to pour into you.

The more you abide in Jesus, the bigger opening you have to receive.

On the other end is the way you add value to others, and it's your confidence that decides the size of the spout.

If you let it, **insecurity will restrict the flow through your life down to a drip.**

You can sit in church every week, listen to worship all day long, read your Bible and pray, and even hear from God, but no fruit will come of it if you lack confidence because **insecurity is the bottleneck.**

The fruit of your life-- the influence, miracles, resources, and love you produce to bless others-- depends on the way you think about yourself.

You were born to bear fruit, but it's not automatic. A fruitful life will require intentional, focused effort to increase your intimacy with God, understand your identity, and develop your confidence.

DAY 144: Psalms 95 - 98

Renewed, Restored, Rejoicing

He preserves the souls of His saints; He delivers them out of the hand of the wicked.

Your mind is designed to operate on light, to overflow with revelation.

Your heart is created to run on gladness, to integrate seamlessly with the heart of God.

Your will is tuned to hate evil and love the Lord.

Your desire is calibrated to greatness, to crave significance and move with ambition.

Jesus came to forgive your sin, heal your body, renew your mind, restore your soul, and awaken your desires.

You are free to believe Him, cooperate with Him, and rule with Him.

Your heart is good.

Your desires are good.

Your nature is good.

Your identity is good.

Your destiny is good.

Live like the gospel works.

DAY 145: Psalms 99 - 102

Serve With Gladness

Serve the LORD with gladness; Come before His presence with singing.

It's not all about you.

As important as it is to believe the truth and love yourself well, you are not the center of the universe.

There is something bigger going on, and someone bigger that started all this.

His agenda, to love the world into wholeness, is what matters most.

You are invited to play a part in His plan, to hold a position of great intimacy and importance.

However, life has a way of overwhelming and distracting you from the incredible opportunity set before you.

It is easy to get lost in the frustration of the mundane.

But there is a solution! **A simple THANK YOU from a sincere heart is like hitting the reset button on your life.**

Before you know it, a song will rise within you, and you'll enter into HIS PRESENCE with a fresh reminder of His incredible goodness.

Serve a mission more significant than yourself. Serve the God who redeemed you. Serve with the awareness of His presence.

Serve the Lord with gladness.

DAY 146: Psalms 103 - 106

Tested By The Word

Until the time that his word came to pass, The word of the LORD tested him.

Joseph had a dream. In his dream, he was a powerful ruler, highly favored, and all of his family bowed down to him. God gave him the dream, and the desire to go with it.

Joseph knew he was destined for greatness-- he had a word from God and the ambition to see it through. But there was a problem; **the word was bigger than he was.**

God needed a man to go ahead of His people, build a relationship with the rulers of Egypt, and prepare the way for His people.

That man needed poise, wisdom, favor, and honor, and would require skill in hearing from God, interpretation, understanding prophetic timing, and leadership.

So God gave a dream to young Joseph, and **that word refined him like gold until it came to pass.**

God put the desire in his heart, a great big crazy desire, and that word led him into the wilderness.

A few years later Joseph came out with not only the experience necessary to govern but incredible maturity in the prophetic. He understood the most challenging aspect to learn-- timing.

You have a word from God, a dream of who you could become.

Stop questioning your word, and let the word test you.

DAY 147: Psalms 107 - 110

Help Me, O Lord My God!

Let them curse, but You bless.

Don't forget, Lord.

Remember every time oppression came against me.

Let every curse spoken against me come before your ears.

May each temptation, attack, and unjust decision never be forgotten.

I am your servant, utterly loyal to your cause!

Help Me!

Let them curse, but You bless.

I will never stop praising You as loud as I can.

Let Your MERCY favor me!

Turn all of the attempts to thwart my progress on the head of my enemy.

Look carefully, O God, at how much I love You and listen to Your voice.

I don't deserve this-- give me justice for every false accusation.

Help me, O Lord my God!

DAY 148: Psalms 111 - 114

Light Arises In The Darkness

Unto the upright there arises light in the darkness.

Jesus made me righteous.

I fear the Lord, and delight greatly in what He says.

I deal graciously and generously with others.

My heart is steadfast, trusting in the Lord.

I am a good person.

My heart is good, my intentions are good, my desires are good.

God is for me-- He speaks, empowers, and blesses me.

If I get distracted or make a mistake, He leads me back on track.

I know, without a doubt, that I am a son of the living God.

Therefore, my descendants will be mighty on the earth.

Wealth and riches will be in my house.

I receive guidance whenever I need it.

I never have to be afraid-- never.

Light always arises in the darkness.

DAY 149: Psalms 115 - 118

I Love The Lord

Return to your rest, O my soul, For the LORD has dealt bountifully with you.

How do you love a God who is LOVE? He doesn't need anything, so what can you give Him that makes a difference?

It is kind of like being a little kid and wondering what to get your Dad for Father's Day. He already has everything He needs and wants, and you don't have any money of your own to spend anyway. Everything you have came from Him, so if you buy Him something, it's like He is buying it for Himself. **There is nothing He needs, but there is a way to make Him happy.** You love the Lord is by getting to know Him and then responding to His nature.

If you know Him as Comforter, you love Him by maintaining REST in your soul.
If you know Him as Father, then you thank Him by living up to the NAME He gave you.
If you know Him as Savior, you appreciate Him by BELIEVING the Gospel and living as if it were true.
If you know Him as Deliverer, you love Him by CALLING on Him when you are in trouble.
If you know Him as the Word, you show gratitude by LISTENING carefully to what He says.
If you know Him as Lord, you thank Him by setting GOALS with Him and following through on your commitments.
If you know Him as Love, you appreciate Him by LOVING others.

Just like any Father, God feels your love when you believe Him and try to emulate Him, and He enjoys watching you live out your calling with dignity and honor.

DAY 150: Psalms 119 - 122

Don't Quit

My help comes from the LORD, Who made heaven and earth.

Don't you dare quit.

I know you are in the fight of your life, battling against the lies that have haunted you forever.

You look in the mirror, and those extra pounds laugh at you.

You avoid checking your bank balance, afraid of what you might see.

You go to bed alone, and you dream of what could be, but then you wake up, still alone.

Your child, who you love more than anything in the world, breaks your heart again.

Sickness mocks you every night, and pain screams at you every morning.

You set goals, but you can never seem to make progress.

Addiction taunts your mind, shouting that you will never amount to anything.

Don't you dare quit. The stakes are too high-- you must win this fight. The world needs you to beat this thing.

Hear the voice of the Father right now cheering you on, "You got this! Relax and breath. Take one step, just one step, in the right direction. Believe one truth. I WILL HELP YOU."

DAY 151: Psalms 123 - 126

Your Soul Is A Fortress

Do good, O LORD, to those who are good, And to those who are upright in their hearts.

Your heart is good.

You are the temple of the Holy Spirit, a dwelling place for God.

Your soul is a fortress, an impenetrable stronghold that the enemy can't reach.

The LORD Almighty surrounds you, protecting you from all harm.

Your confidence, happiness, and focus are entirely under your control.

Nothing can separate you from the Love of God.

You cannot be moved.

Peace covers you.

You are like Mount Zion.

You are a king fellowshipping with the KING.

The Creator protects, loves, blesses, and fights for you.

You are a city set on a hill displayed for all the world to see.

You are the light of the world.

Nobility runs in your veins.

DAY 152: Psalms 127 - 130

Abundant Redemption

O Israel, hope in the LORD; For with the LORD there is mercy, And with Him is abundant redemption.

You should BELIEVE what God says about you.

He thoroughly redeems you, gives you a new name, and speaks creative promises into your life.

The only appropriate response is giddy anticipation of the abundant fruitfulness you are about to experience.

You should be running around like a kid on Christmas sneaking a peek at what is coming soon.

Hope in His WORD!

Anticipate, expect great things, shake the box, and try to guess what an incredible gift God is giving you.

Inside the box is a new life, a fruitful life, and you get to help Him put it together.

Imagine your best self-- you're confident, happy, focused, and living a life of influence, miracles, resources, and love.

Imagine the difference you are making in the lives of others.

He has abundantly redeemed you, and now He is speaking life-giving words to you-- BELIEVE Him!

DAY 153: Psalms 131 - 134

Calm And Quiet

Surely I have calmed and quieted my soul.

I used to want to know why. I wrestled with lofty questions for days, wondering how it could be this way.

Like a hungry baby crying for his mother, life was all about survival. There was no perspective, understanding, or maturity-- there was only need.

I felt helpless and small while I tried to figure out the mysteries of the universe. **I thought that if I could figure out why I would be satisfied,** but it was never enough.

But not anymore-- over the years **I have learned to calm and quiet my soul.** I have learned to live with mystery and faith.

Others don't need to feed me anymore; my heart is my responsibility.

With maturity comes perspective, followed by gratitude.

I don't need a reminder of what God said every five minutes to prop me up-- **I just believe Him.**

He has faithfully shown up again and again, and I will not forget.

There is such peace when you settle into your role and understand your identity. It's not complacency-- you still work hard every day to get better-- but there is rest inside.

I know He will do His job, so all I have to do is mine.

DAY 154: Psalms 135 - 138

Praise From A Whole Heart

In the day when I cried out, You answered me, And made me bold with strength in my soul.

Real appreciation comes not from the needy, but from those who are making an effort to do something great. When you were a kid, you needed your parents, and they did a ton of stuff for you. They provided and protected you the best they could while you sat there helpless.

However, you didn't understand the work and sacrifice involved, so you never fully appreciated what they were doing. If you were anything like me, you complained more than you said thank you. When you grow up, have kids, and realize what it takes, and you're much more grateful.

The same is true in everything. **No one can praise another like the person who has tried to walk in their shoes.**

It's easy to criticize leaders, creators, spokespeople, and business owners while you are sitting on the couch, and it's easy to whine to God when you are sitting in the pew. **Real praise begins when you get in the game and go to work with God.**

Start to cultivate confidence, happiness, and focus, and then use the ideas God gives you to add value to others. He will reveal so much more of Himself, and your worship will go to a whole new level. Grab the microphone, get in front of the camera, take some responsibility, solve a big problem, and love some people deeply, and you will praise differently.

Worship from need is fine, but praise from a whole heart is so much better. It comes from a soul strengthened in the fire of real-life problem solving and dramatic breakthroughs.

DAY 155: Psalms 139 - 142

God Is Thinking Of You

How precious also are Your thoughts to me, O God! How great is the sum of them!

The Creator of the universe is thinking about you right now. He fashioned you with a big dream inside, carefully forming every aspect of your makeup. **He set you up to succeed.**

God hid your identity just below the surface so you could have the joy of discovering it. He is planning your success with extreme attention to detail, and plotting how to invite you into it without violating your self-control.

Your desires and longings are always before Him, and He is well aware of your pain. **You have been wonderfully made.**

The insecurity, emotional brokenness, and stress you struggle with are not the real you, and God has a plan to set you free.

Greatness is in God's heart for you. You are designed to make the world a better place like no one else can. You are not waiting on God to bless you, He already has.

Live aware of His thoughts for you, believing and agreeing with everything He says, taking your brokenness to Him for healing, and focusing your ambition on becoming the best version of yourself.

God is setting you up to win.

Faith is agreeing with God and cooperating with His plan.

Faith is setting yourself up to win.

DAY 156: Psalms 143 - 146

Gracious

The LORD is near to all who call upon Him, To all who call upon Him in truth.

Let's set aside the fact that Jesus is the Creator and commands the honor and respect of every living thing. Ignore for just one second that He is the King that deserves your utmost loyalty. Disregard temporarily the ultimate sacrifice He made to save you from your sin.

Jesus deserves, even demands, absolute duty, honor, respect, obedience, and loyalty, but set those things aside for a minute and consider something else.

He is gracious.

His nature is to give and then give some more. He fills your heart with desire and then helps you fulfill it.

Jesus is the source of all revelation, hope, power, love, and faith. He keeps feeding you with ideas and energy as long as you connect with Him.

Those who fall into the mud He lifts back up. Those with a broken heart He heals and restores. All who look to Him for provision receive it.

He is the vine, the spring, the source of life for every living thing.

Stay connected to Jesus. He deserves it, but don't do it for duty, **do it for love.**

Listen to His voice, stay aware of His presence, make time for Him, meditate on His words, and worship Him in spirit and truth.

You will find grace in your time of need.

DAY 157: Psalms 147 - 150

Praise Is Beautiful

Praise the LORD! For it is good to sing praises to our God; For it is pleasant, and praise is beautiful.

Insecurity is ugly. Doubt and unbelief are hideous. Selfishness, bitterness, and anger are grotesque. Fear and confusion are unsightly.

The heart that is forgiven and restored by God but continues to live controlled by shame and blame is just downright ugly.

Oh, but praise is beautiful.

Praise focuses our attention on the beautiful One-- Jesus. Declaring the greatness of our God is the most beautiful thing we can do, and it makes us attractive.

When we behold Him, we become like Him.

When we pay attention to His kind, generous, and empowering nature, our hearts grow tender, fertile, and fruitful.

Who are the most beautiful people you know?

I bet they are grateful people. More than that, I'm sure they say good things about others to their face and behind their backs.

When you praise, you are making a statement. You are saying, "I am a trusting, thankful, loving, kind, generous, secure, peaceful, and forgiving person."

When you praise, you add a little beauty to the world.

DAY 158: Proverbs 1 - 4

Tend To Your Heart

Keep your heart with all diligence, For out of it spring the issues of life.

Everyone gets one garden to tend. Your heart is your soil, the one acre of ground in the world where you have control.

There is nothing more important than the way you care for that garden-- it is the only way you connect with God, and it is the only way you give life to others.

The way you think about yourself is critical to your success.

If you approach the day thinking like a victim or an orphan, hardened with insecurity, shame, and blame, you will never bear fruit.

But if you confidently reason like the Son or Daughter you are, your influence, miracles, resources, and love will flourish.

Your emotional health, or happiness, determines your depth of growth. Allow your heart to go untended, and fear and anger will keep you shallow, and nothing God says to you will last long enough to make a difference.

Keep your soul free of these boulders through intentional care, and you'll make lasting progress and serve others well.

The desires of your heart, those deep longings to be or do something great, are there for a reason. You need them to grow into a fire of ambition so you can focus and bear fruit. Don't let your desires wither under the stress of financial pressure and busyness-- cultivate and clarify them.

Tend to your soul with diligence-- your fruitfulness depends on it.

DAY 159: Proverbs 5 - 8

Stop Hurting Yourself

But he who sins against me wrongs his own soul; All those who hate me love death."

Most of us agree, in theory, that God loves us and has a meaningful way we can make the world a better place. We also understand that God offers WISDOM on how to live life the best possible way.

Through WISDOM, God teaches us how to excel in our health, relationships, soul care, ministry, education, business, family, finances, and fun.

So here is my question-- **why are so many of us not seeking that WISDOM, or more often, ignoring it?** We know something will benefit our future, but we refuse to do it.

Our lips say God loves us and has a plan for our lives, but our actions are setting us up for disappointment, disease, excuses, confusion, and failure.

Faith believes that your heart is GOOD, that the desires God has put in you are GOOD, and takes steps every day to set yourself up to succeed.

Wisdom says to eat right and exercise, look people in the eyes and listen, keep learning, get enough sleep, cultivate confidence, stop making excuses, and take risks when God speaks.

If we agree with WISDOM, then we love ourselves the way God loves us, and we discipline and encourage ourselves so we can live a fruitful life.

Stop hurting yourself! Discipline yourself today to agree with WISDOM, and **set yourself up to win tomorrow.**

DAY 160: Proverbs 9 - 12

Life-Long Learner

Whoever loves instruction loves knowledge, But he who hates correction is stupid.

Commit to a lifetime of learning. Take the time to gain clarity about who you are on the earth and identify how you add value to others. Then find out the essential skills and subjects that make the most difference.

For me, the critical topics are the Scripture, identity, the prophetic, and fruitfulness. The skills I need are writing, marketing, and public speaking. For you, it will be different because your calling is unique, but the process is the same.

Pick one thing to grow in, and set a goal to master it. The goal needs to be doable but challenging, and attainable within several weeks. (Just long enough to make progress but short enough to stay motivated.)
Find a coach. (Online or in person.), and be willing to pay if necessary.
Start researching, listening, reading, and watching on the topic until you have a decent grasp on the essentials.
Then STOP researching and start PRACTICING.
Keep practicing until you gain some proficiency and get stuck with specific questions, then go back to your coach to find specific answers.
Create necessity every day by thinking about what kind of person you want to be, what feeling you want to have when you reach your goal, how this will benefit others, what rewards you will receive, and the impact it will have on those you love.
Cherish any feedback you get, good or bad, and learn from it.
Discipline and encourage yourself along the way, and then celebrate any progress you make.
After you reach your goal, evaluate your success, mistakes, feedback, and correction. **Then set a new goal, and repeat.**

DAY 161: Proverbs 13 - 16

Increase Or Control?

Where no oxen are, the trough is clean; But much increase comes by the strength of an ox.

The ox teaches us a profound lesson-- you can't have significant increase without relinquishing control.

If you're planting crops, and all you have are your two hands and a hoe, then you can grow about one-fourth of an acre. You can't keep up with any more than that.

If you're a hard worker and a good planner, you can eat most of the year on that, but you'll never have more than you need.

The preparation, plowing, planning, planting, weeding, watering, and harvesting can only be done so fast by yourself.

But throw an ox into the mix, and things start to get interesting.

Plowing and harvesting become much faster with an ox, and you can grow more than you need.

You can sell the excess and hire help, causing your business to prosper. Before you know it, you'll be taking your wife on her dream vacation.

The ox adds tons of value, but it also causes a big mess. **Perfection and control go out the window with an ox.** To increase, you must take risks, clean up messes, trust other people, and make decisions without being 100% sure.

Abundance and perfection can never, ever live in the same house together.

DAY 162: Proverbs 17 - 20

A Deep Well

Counsel in the heart of man is like deep water, But a man of understanding will draw it out.

Our unique life experience, education, and interests combined with the way we hear from God have the potential to change someone else's life, but most of that wisdom never sees the light of day. It's too deep for casual conversation, and we are too busy and stressed to bring it to the surface.

We live next to people who have a solution to our problem, but we never draw it out. We possess answers for the difficulties of others, but we don't bother to sell them on it.

So many people live parched, walking around on the surface in desperate need of counsel, unwilling to draw from the deep well beside us.

But the person of understanding is different-- they refuse to let familiarity stop them from receiving from others. They take time to draw out the best in people in conversation, asking clarifying questions and paying close attention to the answers.

They listen intently to teaching, finding the nuggets of wisdom that can change their life. They are voracious readers, understanding the price someone paid to get that wisdom on the page.

Understanding causes you to draw out the best in others, but it also allows you to offer your best to others.

If we equip, encourage, and empower each other, together we'll change the world.

DAY 163: Proverbs 21 - 24

Pick A Fight

For by wise counsel you will wage your own war, And in a multitude of counselors there is safety.

Time's up.

I'm sorry, but you can't stay here anymore.

I'm DONE!

I'm building a future, and it doesn't involve you.

Whatever you are that keeps me in poverty, alone, ashamed of what I see in the mirror, depressed, and making no impact-- you have got to go.

Insecurity, shame, blame, doubt, pain-- I DECLARE WAR ON YOU!

I will search the Scriptures looking for answers, pray and fast, and listen for God's voice. I will get counsel from my leaders, and pay close attention to it.

I will read every book, take every course, and listen to every message. I will surround myself with wise counsel. Then, it's time to fight.

I will employ every strategy, and remember every testimony.

YOU WILL NOT STAY HERE!

By wise counsel, I will wage war, and I will win.

I WILL WIN.

DAY 164: Proverbs 25 - 28

You Can't Hide Pain

Though his hatred is covered by deceit, His wickedness will be revealed before the assembly.

You burn hot with anger, unable to cool yourself down. Fear grips your mind, choking the life out of you. Hatred and bitterness drive you towards the cliff, trying their best to push you off. Depression weighs you down, covering you with hopelessness.

Strong negative emotions are like boulders in your soul. They make you shallow, shrink your excitement, and demand your attention.

Fear, anger, bitterness, and depression appear as if they've always controlled your heart, but it's not true. They all started as a wound that never got healed.

We all have a standard we live by, a justice system inside of us. Our expectations govern what we feel is right, honest, and fair. When someone breaks those expectations, we feel a deep sense of pain. Something is not right, and we know it. The loss of a loved one, being passed over for a team, being abandoned or abused, or experiencing a traumatic accident can all cause severe wounds in our soul.

We can even hurt ourselves. When we do or say something we did not think we were capable of, it causes the same kind of pain as if another did it to us.

Most of the time, we tell ourselves to suck it up and get it together, but that is NEVER the answer. You can try to pretend like it's not there, but YOU CAN'T HIDE PAIN. Please, take the time to get your wounds healed. Grieve your losses, forgive your enemies, repent for your sins, and let Jesus heal you. **HAPPY is on the other side of healing.**

DAY 165: Proverbs 29 - Ecclesiastes 1

Compensation

It is not for kings to drink wine, Nor for princes intoxicating drink.

Alcohol, drugs, illicit sex, overeating, overspending, impulse shopping, thrill-seeking, entertainment overload-- the list could go on and on. There are so many ways to compensate for our lack of confidence, happiness, and focus. **But why do we do it?**

We're created as kings and queens to add significant value to others. When we think of ourselves that way, as someone with purpose and responsibility, and we take steps to walk out the identity God gave us, then we don't need compensation.

If you refuse to allow insecurity to have a voice in your life, then there's nothing for which to compensate. If you take all of your pain to Jesus for healing, then you don't need to medicate. If you live with focused ambition and make a difference in the world, then you don't need techniques to soothe your anxiety.

Each time we confidently reaffirm our identity, help others, love ourselves well, or focus on priorities we are shouting, "I am a KING!" Kings don't need to compensate; they have everything they need.

On the other hand, **every time you take that drink, make that call, stuff your face, or binge on something harmful you declare to yourself and the world, "I'm a VICTIM!"**

Compensation is for the dying, the bitter, the poor, and the miserable-- **that's not you!** You are a king or queen. You fight for the helpless, get justice for the oppressed, speak up for those with no voice-- you make the world a better place and enjoy doing it.

DAY 166: Ecclesiastes 2 - 5

Fall In Love With The Work

The sleep of a laboring man is sweet.

When you don't have any money, money is a great motivator. When you long for a companion, it's hard to think about anything else.

Most of us live in survival mode, motivated to reach a certain destination. We think that the job, house, friend, money, companion, vacation, promotion, or whatever will satisfy us-- until we get them.

Don't get me wrong, results matter. You need to win the game, get the album released, marry the guy, pay off your debt, or get the job. But once you get what you want it doesn't satisfy as much as you thought, and the motivation wanes the higher up you go.

If you don't have enough money, you think, "I'll get that job or promotion, start that business, sell that thing, or ask that person for help." You may or may not get more money, but either way, **you still need more**. What you should ask is, **"why do I need money?"**

Maybe you lack confidence, skill, leadership ability, knowledge, a degree, or a clear goal. Figure out the real problem, and then be willing to CHANGE, GROW, and WORK HARD to find a real solution.

YOU MUST FALL IN LOVE WITH THE WORK.

Those who love perfecting their craft get MUCH BETTER results than those who love results, and they get to enjoy the process along the way. If you LOVE learning new things, perfecting your skills, and cultivating relationships-- **if you love the work**-- then you will get great results and be satisfied every single day.

DAY 167: Ecclesiastes 6 - 9

A Good Name

A good name is better than precious ointment.

God created you in His image and likeness, and He is a GOOD Father.

You are designed to interact with heaven, restore people's souls, create wealth, and give things meaning and purpose.

You are a Son or Daughter of God-- if you choose to be.

Let me say that again. **Your purpose and identity-- the NAME God gave you-- is yours to choose, or not.**

You must DIE to your selfishness, insecurity, orphan thinking, victim mentality, lustful compensations, and vengeful grudges and be reborn to know who you are.

God will not force you into your destiny; you will walk into it voluntarily, or not at all.

He is setting you up to succeed as we speak.

Will you continue to hold on to your insecurity, pain, and anxiety, or will you answer to the NAME He calls you?

If you surrender the orphan lifestyle, you will lose control, but you will find purpose, fruitfulness, greatness, glory, honor, and the most valuable thing on earth-- a relationship with God.

DAY 168: Ecclesiastes 10 - Song of Songs 1

The Kisses Of His Word

Let him kiss me with the kisses of his mouth--For your love is better than wine.

She took each step with care, placing her feet as if the wood could give way at any moment. Her pace was deliberate, yet cautious, as she neared the center of the bridge. A gentle stream flowed beneath; she could see the water flowing through the gap in the boards.

Intimidated by the distance, she paused, considering the leap she was about to make-- this could end badly. What if it's too far? What if the wood on the other side brakes as she lands? With a deep breath, the young woman steadied herself and leaped across the hole in the bridge. She smiled as she landed, excited she made it. There was a little less care now as she hurried across to the other side.

As soon as she was on dry land off came her shoes, and her bag, and the red scarf around her head. A playful smile brightened her face as the grass tickled her toes. "Finally," she thought. Calling out in a loud but happy voice, the young woman beckoned for her lover, pausing to sing made-up songs between calls. Tan from the long hours in the sun watching the family sheep, the young woman was beautiful, but in a real-life kind of way.

Whenever she could sneak away, she came here, to the secret place her and her lover met. It was a long walk, and a leap of faith across the hole in the rickety bridge to get here, but it was always worth it. "I need to fix that someday," she said out loud to herself, knowing that she never would. Scarf in hand, she danced about, enjoying the soft grass on her feet.

And then, there He was. She smiled, and cried, and stared into His face. **"Talk to me Jesus," she whispered. "Please-- I want to hear everything you have to say."**

DAY 169: Song of Songs 2 - 5

Rise Up

Rise up, my love, my fair one, And come away.

You are Jesus' beloved. He thinks about you all the time and cares about you more than you will ever know.

Jesus genuinely likes your personality, the way you look, the desires you have, and the talents you possess. He enjoys you and never wants you to be like someone else.

Your whole life will change when you believe that the way you talk, give, care, laugh, listen, and love is beautiful to Him.

You'll stop working for forgiveness, acceptance, belonging, and inheritance. You'll quit comparing yourself to others, start enjoying His presence, and become comfortable in your own skin.

But when He asks you to get up and come with Him, do you leave your comfort zone and respond?

Jesus is a man of faith, hope, and love. He's a risk taker, an undying optimist, and a tremendous lover of people.

What He desires-- what He died to make possible-- is a group of people completely in love and equally yoked with Him.

He wants a bride, not an audience.

Jesus longs for an equal partner with the same worldview as Him, that will rise up and follow Him wherever He goes. Will you be His beloved?

DAY 170: Song of Songs 6 - Isaiah 1

Change The Way You Think

"Come now, and let us reason together," Says the LORD, "Though your sins are like scarlet, They shall be as white as snow."

No one can think for you.

You decide to feel like a child of God.

You consider your heart to be good and noble.

Think of yourself as a fruitful branch, firmly grafted into Jesus and bearing much fruit.

Renew your mind until you can demonstrate the will of God on the earth.

Believe that you are the kind of person who does great things with God.

No one controls your mind, not even God. You are free to think as you please.

Seek the clarity you need for the future, and create the necessity to live a fruitful life.

The Father already sent Jesus, unleashed the Holy Spirit, and gave the Word. Jesus already died, rose again, and ascended into heaven.

You've heard the Gospel many times, so **change the way you think and believe that it works, in you, right now.**

Cultivate confidence, pursue wholeness, and get focused. **It's time to start bearing fruit.**

DAY 171: Isaiah 2 - 5

The Kingdom

Come, and let us go up to the mountain of the LORD, To the house of the God of Jacob; He will teach us His ways, And we shall walk in His paths.

Two thousand years ago Jesus changed the course of history, ending the age Moses and establishing a kingdom.

Back then, every government embraced polytheism, satanic rituals, dictatorship, and fear. War was a way of life, and oppression was commonplace.

The kingdom began with only a few hundred devotees spreading the Good News, but after a few decades sharing the message, there was one follower of Jesus to every three hundred people on earth.

Now, **one out of seven** people on earth call on the name of Jesus, and **one hundred thousand a day are added into the kingdom worldwide.**

Many countries' legal systems follow Biblical principles, and most societies expect freedom. The influence of Jesus continues to diminish oppression and violence, while global health and prosperity are at an all-time high.

A worldwide movement of prayer, worship, missions, and miracles continues to grow, and God is speaking to leaders around the globe through His prophets on a regular basis.

When Jesus reigns, things get better; it's impossible for Him to fail.

If you allow Him to influence you, His Spirit will bring confidence, wholeness, and fruitfulness to your world, and you will help bring His peace to those around you.

DAY 172: Isaiah 6 - 9

The King

For unto us a Child is born, Unto us a Son is given; And the government will be upon His shoulder.

Jesus is THE KING.

He is the greater David leading a kingdom right now as you read this.

He laughs at those who think they are in charge, who believe they have a shot at pushing their agenda past His.

Jesus leads like any leader, by influencing people, but unlike most, He has the patience and kindness to allow people to choose Him without bullying.

His influence is growing, and will never stop.

The purpose of His kingdom is to create happy, whole, healthy, prosperous, and free people who know the Father intimately and love each other intentionally.

You can't stop Him, but you can join Him.

If you submit under His authority and commit to loving His people, He will anoint and appoint you to help change the world.

Change the way you think and believe that THE King made you a king, and join Him in making the earth look like heaven.

DAY 173: Isaiah 10 - 13

The Rod Of His Mouth

But with righteousness He shall judge the poor, And decide with equity for the meek of the earth; He shall strike the earth with the rod of His mouth, And with the breath of His lips He shall slay the wicked.

Jesus came to end the age of Moses, in which people tried to follow God by keeping the law and offering sacrifices. The laws were not bad, nor was the system-- it was just incomplete. It dealt with the outward actions of people, not the heart, **allowing people to look righteous, but inwardly be corrupt.**

Jesus changed all that, establishing a New Covenant that works from the inside out. No longer is there a physical temple, city, and sacrifice, nor does following an outward list of rules qualify you for a reward.

Jesus used THE ROD OF HIS MOUTH to set the standard and decide who is righteous. He wrote the rules on our hearts, empowering believers to prosper while religious pretenders disqualify themselves. God now only accepts worship done in Spirit and truth, so **the condition of your heart determines your access.**

If you listen to Jesus' words, understand them, and obey what He says, then you judge yourself worthy. But if you harden your heart like a victim, hold on to your brokenness, and allow stress to choke out God's words, you judge yourself unworthy of a new heart, the Holy Spirit, and eternity with the Creator.

Jesus' WORDS, draw a perfect line in the sand that allows each person who hears them decide their fate. **Genius.**

DAY 174: Isaiah 14 - 17

The Orphan Spirit

For you have said in your heart: "I will ascend into heaven, I will exalt my throne above the stars of God."

Ever wonder why the enemy is always trying to make you feel like an orphan?

His temptations drone on and on with nonsense like, "God is disappointed in you" or "you blew it now" or "just forget it, you'll never amount to anything." Satan and his crowd keep trying to get you to question the heart of the Father.

God says, "You are my beloved son, in whom I am well pleased," while the enemy pines on and on with the question, "Are you sure God likes you?"

If he can get you to spend your life attempting to earn what God desires to give you for free, you'll get stuck in the wilderness your whole life. **The devil is the ultimate orphan.** He had a home near the heart of God, but he threw it away in an attempt to launch out on his own.

If you listen to the enemy of your soul, your heart will become hardened with a victim mentality as you work, steal, manipulate, lie, and scrap your whole life for acceptance when you could have merely believed for it.

Don't let that wiley orphan get you to join him in the fight for approval.

Believe in the Son and rest in the arms of the Father who created you, and put all of your efforts into working with God to bring wholeness to the people around you.

DAY 175: Isaiah 18 - 21

Learning To See

For thus has the Lord said to me: "Go, set a watchman, Let him declare what he sees."

Practice.

Success always comes down to practice.

What is true in sports, music, and business also applies to your awareness and understanding of what God is doing and saying.

You may receive an impartation from great leaders, desire earnestly spiritual gifts, and keep asking for more.

You can read the books, go to seminars, and listen intently to teachers.

All of that stuff is helpful, and you should do it, but nothing can replace practice.

Trial and error, patience, and persistence teach you things you can't learn any other way.

If you want to see in the spirit and understand what you are seeing, then sign up for the long game and fall in love with the work.

Confidence is built alone in the gym shooting hundreds of shots after everyone else has gone home.

Repetition is the only path to mastery.

DAY 176: Isaiah 22 - 25

Removing The Veil

And He will destroy on this mountain The surface of the covering cast over all people, And the veil that is spread over all nations.

There is a veil that covers the mind of nearly every person you know. It's like a pair of tinted glasses, distorting the way people see the world. The veil is called an **orphan spirit**, and it affects everyone not yet sons and daughters of God.

With those glasses on the world looks pretty dark, and feels cold. There is no sense of belonging, so you give in to peer pressure trying to fit in. There is no absolute right or wrong, so you wander around in the land of relativity, wondering which way to go.

Purpose, identity, and forgiveness, the things only the Father can give, do not exist, so you grope around in the dark for meaning.

Orphan glasses cause you to see the world through the lens of selfishness and survival, leaving you with only one option-- to fend for yourself.

But Jesus, the glorious One, is a SON above all else; He is fully committed to the will of the Father. He is the King, the Savoir, the Sacrifice, and the High Priest, but at His core, He is a Son.

When you believe in Jesus and start following Him, you become a son or daughter as well. The cold, hard world in which you must scrap for yourself lights up with love and acceptance.

Put on your SON glasses today and see a world where belonging and forgiveness are free, where the only work is loving others into wholeness with the Father.

DAY 177: Isaiah 26 - 29

Perfect Peace

You will keep him in perfect peace, Whose mind is stayed on You, Because he trusts in You.

You can't generate peace on your own, it comes with the presence of the Holy Spirit. But you can control how you think, and God promises that if you keep your mind right, He will give you a lifetime subscription to peace.

Many of us, however, don't believe we have control over our minds. We succumb to a victim mentality and allow our peace to get stolen.

But you are not a victim!

Neither God, the devil, or other people control your life-- **you manage yourself.**

What we call trust is often a victim mentality.

We say that we're "trusting in God" when in reality we're hoping that He will motivate us, control our mind for us, develop our skills, cultivate our confidence, and force us to succeed.

We make ourselves a slave of "God's will" because we do not believe what He says about us. If He places a desire in your heart or gives you a prophetic word, you should run with it.

God is not going to believe for you, motivate you, build your confidence, let go of your anger, focus your mind, or make you prosper. He will speak to you, give you grace, forgive you, heal you, and pour out the Holy Spirit on you in direct proportion to the self-control you exercise over your mind.

DAY 178: Isaiah 30 - 33

The Difference Maker

Until the Spirit is poured upon us from on high, And the wilderness becomes a fruitful field, And the fruitful field is counted as a forest.

Before Christ, every family blessed by God had a piece of property as their inheritance.

As they followed God's principles, their land prospered, but if they neglected His ways, the ground became unfruitful.

But Jesus switched things up, giving you a good and noble heart to cultivate and direct access to heaven through the Holy Spirit.

Now, you develop your soul with God as your business partner, hoping to produce things that add value to others.

Don't underestimate the difference one person can make with the help of the Holy Spirit!

When you accept responsibility for your thoughts, feelings, and desires and cooperate with Him fully, anything is possible.

Through the Holy Spirit, you have access to unlimited revelation, grace, gifts, power, and love-- everything you need to prosper, stay healthy, and impact the world around you.

Cooperate with Him, listen to Him, follow his lead, and embrace His help.

Lean heavily on THE DIFFERENCE MAKER, and you will be amazed at the results.

DAY 179: Isaiah 34 - 37

Be Strong, Do Not Fear!

Be strong, do not fear! Behold, your God will come with vengeance, With the recompense of God; He will come and save you.

Jesus is near. He didn't lie to you, and He will never abandon you.

Be strong. I don't mean suck it up and wait like a victim. I mean, BE STRONG! Take risks, be courageous, cultivate confidence and do something!

Live as if every word God said to you is guaranteed to happen.

Do not fear.

No, I'm not trying to comfort you in your unbelief. I'm saying don't allow yourself one minute to imagine "what if" scenarios. Don't let yourself be afraid. Feed yourself on prophecies and testimonies, and prepare yourself for the breakthrough.

God has judged in your favor!

You're not the victim here, the enemy is. You are binding the strong man on the inside right now so you can take his stuff and stomp on his head.

QUIT acting like a victim!

The eyes of the blind shall see, the ears of the deaf shall open, the lame shall leap like a deer, and the tongue of the dumb shall sing. Water is about to burst forth in the wilderness, and streams will flow in the desert.

DAY 180: Isaiah 38 - 41

Wait On The Lord

Why do you say, O Jacob, And speak, O Israel: "My way is hidden from the LORD, And my just claim is passed over by my God"?

God rewards those who diligently seek Him-- every time. So, if you're in a "waiting" season, saying stuff like, "My way is hidden from the LORD, And my just claim is passed over by my God," then you adopted a victim mentality somewhere along the way.

Jesus paid an immeasurable price for you to have a relationship with God and partner with Him to bless others.

The victim-minded waiting most of us think we are in is for those who still think they are earning their acceptance, forgiveness, favor, approval, and anointing. **Real waiting, as referred to in Isaiah 40, is what a worker feels doing their job and EXPECTING to get paid at the end of the day.** They may not have the cash in hand yet, but they are confident they will when the time comes.

God made it crystal clear that you have His approval and He means every word He says. **So, if you're "waiting" for Him to prove that He likes you and has a purpose for your life, you'll be waiting forever.** There is nothing left for Him to do to convince you of that. Every minute of every day God is actively setting you up to succeed. He is comforting, coaching, forgiving, healing, and empowering you to live the most fulfilling life possible.

STOP working and waiting for Him to prove His love for you, and start working with Him to DO YOUR JOB. Renewed strength is for those in the trenches every day, expecting a reward for their efforts to make the world a better place.

DAY 181: Isaiah 42 - 45

What's Your Name?

Another will write with his hand, 'The LORD's,' And name himself by the name of Israel.

When it's just you, alone in your room, what do call yourself?

What do you want to be known for?

When God thinks about you, and believe me He does, **what should He call you?**

Your mom and dad are responsible for your first and last name, so you didn't have a choice in the matter.

Over the years you picked up nicknames and titles, names that others call you. Some of them were good, and some not so hot.

Your kids call you one thing and your grandkids something else.

But what do you call yourself? Or, more importantly, what name do you answer to?

When the Spirit of God is coursing through your veins, something changes inside.

You begin to embrace who you are and self-identify as SON or DAUGHTER. You accept your role on the team, and you start to feel like you belong.

I'm sorry, but I don't answer to Victim anymore, or Orphan, or Lonely, or Insecure. I AM THE LORD'S.

DAY 182: Isaiah 46 - 49

Kings Shall Arise

I will preserve You and give You As a covenant to the people, To restore the earth, To cause them to inherit the desolate heritages.

How would you live if you were one hundred percent convinced that Jesus came to restore the earth, and you are the means through which He's doing it?

What would your life look like if you believed that not only is your heart GOOD, but that you are a KING on the earth? I don't mean in theory, I mean for real.

LIVE AS IF THE GOSPEL IS TRUE!

God loves you, and He is setting you up to succeed. He called you to bear much fruit, to live with influence, miracles, resources, and love.

The restoration of the earth is in your hands.

When you see Jesus as He is, you must see yourself as a KING, and you must ARISE. You have full access to the Spirit of God. That means you can recover from any pain, learn whatever you need to know, and solve any problem.

STOP living to pay bills-- choose a group of people to bless and a problem to solve, and the money will follow.

Cultivate clarity, confidence, wholeness, and focus, and refuse to live in shame or blame. Live as if God is real, He loves you, He has already restored you, and now He is empowering you to help restore the earth.

DAY 183: Isaiah 50 - 53

I Will Not Be Ashamed

For the Lord GOD will help Me; Therefore I will not be disgraced; Therefore I have set My face like a flint, And I know that I will not be ashamed.

I will do anything to finish the mission. **I have set my face like a flint-- nothing will deter me.**

Because of my resolve to be who God created me to be and do His will, I get access to inside information.

Clarity, confidence, happiness, and focus are mine to develop, and I will cultivate them with care.

The Father continually teaches me how to talk to those who need my help, and I pay close attention. Every day I wake up hearing His voice in my ear, training me in the ways of wisdom.

My ability to receive revelation and speak with influence is on par with the most brilliant thought leaders, and I never stop improving.

I submit to the will of the Father-- I will not shy away from His polarizing message or the inevitable rejection.

I will not control my life to keep it small; I say yes to greatness.

God will help me, of that I am sure. He started this and invited me to participate, and now He will help me finish strong.

I refuse to let shame have a voice in my life, nor will I ever blame anyone for the state of my heart. I'm all in-- there is no going back now.

DAY 184: Isaiah 54 - 57

Enlarge Your Place

Enlarge the place of your tent, And let them stretch out the curtains of your dwellings; Do not spare; Lengthen your cords, And strengthen your stakes.

For you shall expand to the right and the left. How does that statement make you feel?

If you have more money, influence, anointing, property, or people, you get more responsibility-- there's no way around it.

And yet, God embedded in your heart to want more, to expand and bear much fruit. God is glorified when you enlarge your sphere of influence to impact more people-- and so are you.

We were designed to continually grow, bear fruit, and make a significant difference in the world. So why don't we? **Control.**

To marry an influential person, you must let them be who they are. To grow an organization, you must develop leaders who may do things a little different than you. To expand a business, you must stop controlling everything, focus on what you do best, and help others thrive.

Control keeps things small, allowing us to manage them without confronting our internal weaknesses. **Control lets you stay in your comfort zone.**

But God gets no glory when you restrict growth to stay comfortable. He made you to stretch, to keep influencing more people in significant ways.

Choose to enlarge, stretch, and expand. Don't let control restrict the fruit of your life.

DAY 185: Isaiah 58 - 61

Arise, Shine!

Arise, shine; For your light has come! And the glory of the LORD *is risen upon you.*

"Jesus, whenever you're ready, shine your light in the darkness! Send revival, release healing, change the culture, bring reconciliation-- we need you!"

Doesn't God live inside us? Didn't He already send Jesus? Hasn't the cross, resurrection, ascension, and outpouring of the Holy Spirit already taken place? Do we not have the Bible plus two thousand years of prophecies and testimonies from which to draw?

What are we waiting for?

You are the light of the world. Arise, and shine.

You seek clarity about your calling.

You cultivate confidence. You learn to stay happy and whole.

You create necessity and focus.

You bear fruit.

You develop deep relationships. You master your craft.

You learn to interpret what God is saying to you.

You build a platform of influence.

You are the light of the world. Arise, and shine.

DAY 186: Isaiah 62 - 65

The Lord Delights In You

As the bridegroom rejoices over the bride, So shall your God rejoice over you.

The anticipation. The excitement. The nervousness.

Is there anything that gets the heart pounding more than a bridegroom marrying his bride?

My wife and I dated for a couple of years before we got married, and we waited for physical intimacy until after the wedding. We didn't even kiss until our wedding day.

The whole process-- the awkwardness of the first date, the excitement of thinking she may be the one, the agony of figuring out if I should commit the rest of my life to her, and the anticipation of an eight-month-long engagement-- culminated on one October day when we said yes to each other.

I was excited, nervous, and relieved.

The waiting and wondering were finally over, and I rejoiced in knowing that I had someone to love who loved me back.

That is how God feels about you.

Thinking of you lights Him up, and He can't wait to share His life with you.

You make Him smile and sing, and He is fully committed to setting you up to succeed. Never forget-- you are LOVED, ENJOYED, and ANTICIPATED. You make the Creator REJOICE.

DAY 187: Isaiah 66 - Jeremiah 3

On Purpose

Before I formed you in the womb I knew you.

I am not an accident. I did not evolve from a monkey, or form from the magic dust of the universe. My loving Father fashioned me in His image to work with Him in the family business.

The orphan spirit screams in my ear, "You're not wanted! You have no purpose! You blew it again! You're an accident! God doesn't know you! Nobody knows you! You're the only one! Prove your worth, if you have any!"

Nope, not today-- I'm not going to listen to a word you say. I've got nothing to prove. While I rest in the arms of my Father, let me tell you something. **I didn't form myself, God did.** Matter of fact, I didn't save, forgive, heal, or call myself either. God accepted me when I was clueless, named me and gave me purpose-- **all I did was say yes.**

So while you spit your orphan and victim garbage at me, begging me to agree with you, I'm going to sit here at my Daddy's table and rest. You're the one with something to prove. You had it made and chose to throw it all away. So keep your garbage-- I'll pass.

God knew me before He ever created me. He formed me to be just like Him: creative, loving, intentional, bold, and kind. **I'm fine with submission, faith, and obedience.** I don't mind sitting here in the warmth of His love, feeding on His goodness, and telling others what He tells me to say.

You go ahead and stay out in the cold fending for yourself and trying to manipulate everyone you see. I'm good right here, **resting on purpose.**

DAY 188: Jeremiah 4 - 7

Break Up The Fallow Ground

Break up your fallow ground, And do not sow among thorns.

For some reason, I always thought fallow ground meant hard, unusable soil that needed some serious rehabilitation, but that's not what it means at all. Fallow ground is soil that has the potential to bear fruit but is unused right now.

God's advice to His people is, "Stop wasting your potential. I keep giving you answers, ideas, wisdom, promises, prophetic direction, and understanding, but so little of what I am saying ever bears fruit."

Insecurity robs our fruitfulness, causing us to discount God's ideas because we feel inadequate to grow them. Brokenness crowds out our growth by overshadowing the dreams God gives us with fear, anger, or depression. Stress buries our potential by demanding our constant attention. We run from fire to fire trying to keep things contained, staying busy but accomplishing nothing.

If you have an acre of ground to plant corn, but you only plant four rows, what does that say about you? The fruitful life is the ALL IN life. Go BIG in everything you do, focus on one thing at a time, refuse to blame, pursue excellence, and maximizing your potential.

The fruitful life is believing that your heart is so good that God would never tell you anything that was not vitally important, and meticulously cultivating the confidence, wholeness, and focus necessary to grow His ideas.

So break up your fallow ground. Go ALL IN and sow the words of God in every inch of your heart, expecting a massive return on investment.

DAY 189: Jeremiah 8 - 11

Glory In Knowing Him

But let him who glories glory in this, That he understands and knows Me.

You should pursue wisdom, health, and productivity with all your might, but they should never become the source of your confidence.

To live a life of influence and honor is a noble endeavor, and you should pursue it.

But your wealth, intelligence, and fitness should not be what you're known for-- **people should recognize the glory of God on your life.**

Your ability to understand and know God, and demonstrate His passion for people, is the only thing worthy of honor.

Get to know God so well that you talk and act like Him, and represent His love, judgment, and righteousness everywhere you go.

You should feel proud of yourself at the end of each day.

While you're lying in bed at night, contemplating your day, you should feel good about what you accomplished.

But it's not about the size of the crowd, the money in the bank, or the awards on your shelf.

Your sense of accomplishment must come from knowing God, understanding what He is doing, and cooperating with Him as He loves people into wholeness.

Glory in the fact that you think, act, talk, feel, and love like God.

DAY 190: Jeremiah 12 - 15

Line Upon Line

Thus the LORD said to me: "Go and get yourself a linen sash, and put it around your waist, but do not put it in water."

Can I just come out and say it? You have a problem. You're still seeking affirmation from God instead of believing you already have it. It's a problem because when God speaks, the only question on your mind is, "do you like me now?" making every word from God a test of one of two things: are you messing up or is He making you wait.

But God doesn't want to talk about that stuff anymore; He already proved that He loved you long ago. He wants to talk about how to love people into wholeness, serve people at a higher level, solve more significant problems, and walk in a greater anointing. To do that, He must build line upon line, precept upon precept, teaching you one lesson at a time. **As long as you're still wondering if He likes you every time He talks, you start the conversation over from the beginning, making progress impossible.**

A few years ago I was praying, and I felt led to go to a conference in California. As I pursued it, God supernaturally provided the finances, and we had a life-changing experience. Upon my return, I got the inspiration to write a book. I set a ten-week goal to finish it, and I was able to publish my first book around my birthday the same year I attended the conference. After dealing with the emotions of releasing a book, I realized I didn't know how to sell it. One thing kept leading to the other, and I followed the desires and instructions God gave me into starting an online business.

My point is, the question is not, "Do you like me now?" it's, "How do we make people's lives better?" If that is what you're asking, God will continue to lead you line by line into greater love, influence, miracles, resources, and anointing.

DAY 191: Jeremiah 16 - 19

Inherited Lies

The Gentiles shall come to You From the ends of the earth and say, "Surely our fathers have inherited lies, Worthlessness and unprofitable things."

Evolution. The sexual revolution. Religious pretense. A victim mentality. Hopelessness. Poverty. Racism. Relativism. **I bet you inherited some lies.**

It could be from the culture you live in, or the family you grew up with, but more than likely, you were taught something that has hurt you. That's why the gospel starts with repentance, then you renew your mind, He restores your soul, and His Spirit empowers your spirit.

But how do you get someone who is entrenched in lies to believe the truth? Most of us try prayer, serving, comfort, teaching, or arguing, but the results are usually sub-par because of our God-given free will.

The way we think about ourselves drives our actions, so we must self-identify as a particular kind of person before we can consistently act like one-- **there is no way to make yourself do something that is opposite of the way you think about yourself.**

So, the ONLY WAY to get someone to change their behavior is for them to change the way they think voluntarily, and the ONLY WAY to get them to do that is to SELL.

"Follow Me," Jesus said, after making sure people knew the price they would pay to do so. Some hated Him and some adored Him, but He utterly transformed everyone who believed. Don't allow the lies you inherited to continue to define you. Go all-in, buy the truth, and self-identify as a son or daughter of God. **Then SELL like crazy.**

DAY 192: Jeremiah 20 - 23

All I Do Is Win

"Is not My word like a fire?" says the LORD, "And like a hammer that breaks the rock in pieces?"

"That's just the way I am. I don't know how. I don't have time. I could never do that. I'm scared. I'm just not good at that. It's too painful. I tried that before." Really? How do you let yourself think like that? Seriously, why would you volunteer to feel like a victim?

Don't we serve the God that created the universe? Isn't He madly in love with you? Hasn't He already done everything necessary for you to live happy, free, whole, and powerful?

Think about the excuses you are making. You could never, ever do that thing because it's too hard, right? Now, imagine someone promised you a million dollars if you did it? What if they guaranteed that it would set your kids, grandkids, and great-grandkids up to succeed for generations to come?

How about if doing it would change thousands of lives forever? Imagine standing before the Lord, face to face, and Him saying you did a great job. What if you were promised a happy, healthy, and meaningful life? **Would you do it?**

All of that stuff IS waiting on the other side of doing hard things.

God told Jeremiah, "I don't even know what it is to fail. All I do is win, every time. My word ALWAYS works. Every person who has ever agreed with and obeyed My voice has succeeded."

Are you sure you are the only exception? Are you sure you want to play the victim? Are you sure you want to make excuses?

DAY 193: Jeremiah 24 - 27

A Heart To Know God

Then I will give them a heart to know Me, that I am the LORD; and they shall be My people, and I will be their God, for they shall return to Me with their whole heart.

We tend to promote improvement.

"Read your Bible more, go to church more, pray more, eat better, exercise, stop acting like that, and start doing this," we say to ourselves and others.

But the Gospel is different.

Jesus says, "Everything you heard before is incomplete. Leave everything and FOLLOW ME. Go ALL-IN, put all your trust in what I'm saying, and identify yourself as My disciple."

If I say, "I'm a world-changer. I believe every word Jesus says, without proof, just because He said it. My heart is good, and I am custom made to solve a problem," forming the right habits is easy.

Self-identifying as a world changer comes first-- the rest is just details.

Stop trying to improve your behavior.

Believe that your heart is whole and good because Jesus made it that way, not based on your track record. You didn't redeem yourself, Jesus did, so stop arguing with Him.

Change the way you think about yourself, and the habits will follow.

Spend your energy cultivating your identity and learning to rest in God's purpose for your life.

DAY 194: Jeremiah 28 - 31

The New Covenant

I will put My law in their minds, and write it on their hearts; and I will be their God, and they shall be My people.

When God made a New Covenant with His people, He went all-in by committing the life of His only begotten Son to build a relationship with you.

Your role in the relationship is simple: BELIEVE and CONFESS. Believe that the covenant is real, that Jesus is the only way to get to the Father, and that whatever God says is a done deal. Then go public by agreeing out loud that Jesus is your Lord and start following Him.

Once you do that, it's God's turn. His role is massive: completely forgive all your sin as if it never happened, adopt you into the family, give you a brand new heart that is predisposed to do right, and fill you with His Spirit.

It's this simple: God says you're awesome, you believe Him, and then you say, "I'm amazing." Then you start thinking and acting like it's true.

"But I don't feel awesome. Look at what I did the other day, that proves I'm messed up." So, your so-called "evidence" trumps what God said? Therein lies the problem.

Proving yourself is the old covenant, and it doesn't work because your actions will always align with your identity.

So, let's go back to the New Covenant. If you will believe that your heart is good and raise your hand and say, "I'm a son," then God changes your heart and starts talking to you. That's all you need to change the world.

DAY 195: Jeremiah 32 - 35

Motivated By Fear

And I will make an everlasting covenant with them, that I will not turn away from doing them good; but I will put My fear in their hearts so that they will not depart from Me.

Perfect love casts out all fear. **Except for one.**

We all stand before THE KING and answer for the choices we make. I don't know about you, but it scares me when He asks, "Do you believe My words? Do you love My people? Are you maximizing the potential I gave you?"

Jesus is alive, He is THE KING, and He is building a kingdom. He gives each of us assignments to add value to His people, and He expects us to follow through. **Remember when Jesus called that guy who buried his talent a wicked and lazy servant? Yeah, that scares me.** If I don't take what God gives me and double it, I run the risk of losing it, and worse than that, disappointing Jesus.

"But I don't like the pressure. I hate feeling the weight of expectations. Can't we just sing and be nice and pat each other on the back?" **You can, but you're missing a huge source of motivation.**

God said to Jeremiah, "I will put My fear in their hearts so that they will not depart from Me." The fear of God is a crucial ingredient for staying on the right path.

When all other motivation wanes, the fear of the Lord will keep you on track. There are only a few sources of motivation-- the fear of loss, the desire for reward, our sense of identity, the fear of God, and our love for others-- and we need them all to reach our full potential.

DAY 196: Jeremiah 36 - 39

Compassion

But Nebuzaradan the captain of the guard left in the land of Judah the poor people, who had nothing, and gave them vineyards and fields at the same time.

Results come from habits, habits come from actions, actions come from feelings, and feelings come from our thoughts.

Usually, when we want different results, we try to bully ourselves into acting better, forgetting that our feelings are our greatest motivation.

Next time, try something new-- **have compassion on yourself.** Don't make excuses or give up, just **take the time to understand why you act a certain way.**

To change the way you think, you must begin with the assumption that Jesus made your heart good. Then set yourself up to succeed by finding a model, listening to encouraging speakers, and cultivating the confidence and motivation to act.

Imagine how you will feel while you're doing the thing you want to do, then celebrate when you make progress. Invest money on things that propel you forward, and forgive yourself if you mess up.

Be kind to yourself.

Change is hard. To do it well, you need a model, encouragement, motivation, training, inspiration, and accountability.

Have compassion on yourself. Set yourself up to win by giving your mind what it needs to produce positive feelings, actions, habits, and results.

DAY 197: Jeremiah 40 - 43

Be Patient

And it happened after ten days that the word of the LORD came to Jeremiah.

He is one of the greatest prophets of all time.

God trusted Him with some of the most challenging words to deliver ever, and he faithfully stewarded God's trust.

Jeremiah was a true prophet of God.

Some good people came to him with a reasonable request to pray for them, and God answered with an affirming word-- **ten days later**.

We know that Jeremiah could hear from God, the request made was legitimate, and God wanted to answer, but it still took some time.

We don't know why it took that long, and we probably never will.

You don't have to second-guess yourself every time there is a delay, just be patient.

God is for you one hundred percent.

He is setting you up to succeed.

He will speak to you, a little at a time, according to your willingness to ask, seek understanding about what you hear, and follow through.

But it may take awhile. **There's no rush-- fall in love with the process, the work, and the relationship with Him, not just the results.**

DAY 198: Jeremiah 44 - 47

Pursue Your Promises

Jacob shall return, have rest and be at ease; No one shall make him afraid.

When God makes a promise, the fulfillment of that promise is contingent upon you believing Him.

He told Jeremiah that the offspring of Israel would return from their captivity and have rest back in their homeland.

Do you know how God fulfilled that promises? **He spoke.**

He spoke to Daniel to pray, and to Cyrus, the Persian king, to pay for the whole thing.

He spoke to Ezra and Nehemiah to lead, and to Zechariah and Haggai to prophesy. He told the people to go back and get to work.

If you're waiting for God to do more than speak, you're going to keep waiting.

To get your breakthrough, you must believe Him when He speaks, overcome your fear, and pursue with all your might the thing He promised. God will not do it for you.

He will speak to you, and if your heart is ready, His word will grow into fruitful action.

But if you're waiting on Him to cultivate your confidence, overcome your fear, make you focus, or do your job-- **well, that may be why you are still waiting instead of walking into your promise.**

DAY 199: Jeremiah 48 - 51

Transitions

Come and let us join ourselves to the LORD In a perpetual covenant That will not be forgotten.

In Jeremiah's day, Babylon was invincible. They came through the land crushing everything in sight and took the people of Israel captive.

God told Jeremiah that within a few decades Babylon would fall and that during that time Israel would seek the Lord, and it all happened just like the prophet predicted.

If you have lived long enough, you too have faced hardship. Tragedy, loss, betrayal, sin, addiction, or divorce may have left you feeling like a victim.

Perhaps you feel stuck in some area, unable to see a way out.

Motivation, clarity, confidence, and focus can be hard to come by when you feel trapped, but God is showing you how to change.

Use your transitions to seek the Lord.

When there is a significant change in your life, with it comes new grace to change your heart.

New jobs, moving, leaving the house, a parent passing on, a boss or pastor transitioning, a promotion or graduation offers the chance for a fresh start.

During the transition, let the tears flow, and seek the Lord. Ask Him the way forward, and make a new commitment to serve Him with all your heart. Hold nothing back. Use the transition in your life to create lasting change in your heart.

DAY 200: Jeremiah 52 - Lamentations 3

Consider Your Destiny

She did not consider her destiny; Therefore her collapse was awesome.

There are two fundamental approaches to life.

The first one looks at life as a lottery.

If you were born with good genes, grew up in a healthy family, and attracted the right guy or girl, then life goes well. If not, you're stuck with the left-overs.

I think you know where I stand on that theory-- **it's complete garbage.**

The other outlook on life is the exact opposite.

Everyone has a unique destiny and purpose given to you by God. You and only you can fulfill that destiny, and if you don't, no one will.

God adores you, thinks about you often, speaks empowering words to you daily, and sets you up to succeed.

But your success is not contingent on God; it's your choice.

By embracing the lottery mindset, you're ignoring your destiny. You're assigning control of your life to another, and setting yourself up to fail.

However, if you seek clarity about who God created you to be, cultivate the confidence and motivation to act, pursue emotional wholeness, and focus your efforts on your calling, you will succeed.

You must BELIEVE in the destiny God gave you and pursue it every day.

DAY 201: Lamentations 4 - Ezekiel 2

Empowered

Then the Spirit entered me when He spoke to me.

Here's how to sabotage yourself and remain stuck in survival mode:

Assume that there's something wrong with you that will take a long time to fix, live as if you are waiting on God, and ignore the impressions God gives you as unimportant because you think you are insignificant.

Give everything a half-hearted try so you can have an excuse when it doesn't work, blame others, God, the devil, or circumstances for your lack of progress, and bully yourself with shame when you mess up.

Sound familiar? It doesn't have to be that way.

The words God speaks to us come with the Spirit who empowers us to fulfill them, **but you must BELIEVE.**

Believe you are the perfect person to receive what God is saying, your heart is good and noble, and that now is the best time to act.

Believe God is already setting you up to succeed, you can learn anything you need to know, and then go all-in to fulfill His purpose for your life.

When you receive what God is saying with a believing heart, the Spirit empowers you to accomplish it. **Stop pretending that you are "working on" doing what God said when we both know you are sabotaging yourself every chance you get.** If you are looking for excuses to fail, you will find them, but if you seek the Spirit's help to fulfill your calling, receive what God is saying with a believing heart.

DAY 202: Ezekiel 3 - 6

God's Broken Heart

I was crushed by their adulterous heart which has departed from Me.

That still, small voice of God keeps whispering to me, "every time you believe Me for something, it happens." I argued with Him at first, citing my case studies in which I didn't see results, but eventually, I gave up. I gave up because I realized He was right-- **He's always right.**

I've lived most of my life in the wilderness, clinging to grasshopper thinking while waiting on God to prove Himself to me. **I acted as if I wanted His promises, but affirmation is what I was really after.**

God kept saying, "don't be afraid," but **I thought it was a suggestion to encourage me.** I thought was faith a feeling or a mental agreement with some theory, but I was wrong.

Faith is the way Joshua and Caleb reasoned when spying out the promised land, how David acted against Goliath, and how Jesus talked to Satan in the wilderness.

Faith demands that you change the way you think, talk, and act-- and **it always works**. It is a burning fire of belief that operates without proof.

I'm sorry God for keeping my life small because I preferred excuses over results. **I don't want to break your heart any longer with my half-hearted life.**

Make me great, and set me up as an example. Take away all my excuses, shame, fear, blame, insecurity, and small thinking.

The wilderness is overrated-- **let's pick a fight with some giants.**

DAY 203: Ezekiel 7 - 10

What You Do In The Dark

"Son of man, do you see what they are doing, the great abominations that the house of Israel commits here, to make Me go far away from My sanctuary?"

Your mind is the temple of the living God, and your emotions are His dwelling place.

Your physical body hosts God's presence, and your desires and decisions either invite Him to stay with you or drive Him away.

The world between your ears determines whether God manifests His presence in and through you-- or not.

God asked Ezekiel, **"Have you seen what the elders of Israel do in the dark?"**

Well, the physical temple is no more; God resides inside of us now. What you do in the dark-- your thoughts, feelings, desires, and decisions-- connect you to God, allowing Him to act in and through you. Previous generations referred to it as the ancient paths, teaching us that nothing was more important than our secret life with God.

So, how is your inner life?

Are worship, gratitude, compassion, ambition, confidence, and happiness your normal state?

God is attracted to those who practice courage and compassion on the inside when no one is looking. Attract the presence of God in the dark-- and He will reward you in the light.

DAY 204: Ezekiel 11 - 14

Known In Heaven

"Even if these three men, Noah, Daniel, and Job, were in it, they would deliver only themselves by their righteousness," says the Lord GOD.

Israel was in serious trouble. Decades of idolatry, abusing the poor, conspiring with the enemy, and breaking God's heart landed them in a position where correction was the only option.

However, while He was talking to Ezekiel about the future of His people, God said that even if Noah, Daniel, and Job were still in the land and asked for mercy, that their presence and prayers would only save themselves. Isn't that fascinating?

The implications are that God would usually relent if a righteous person asked Him to, but the violations of the people were so severe that they could not go unpunished. But what stands out most is **God mentioned three guys by name.**

Job and Noah lived long ago and were considered the most righteous people of their generation, but Daniel was still alive while God was talking to Ezekiel.

How cool is that? God implied Daniel was such an incredible person that He considered relenting from His plan to punish Israel even though they fell deep into demon worship for decades and needed correction. Wow!

God honored Daniel, mentioning him by name while he was still alive, calling him a righteous man, and giving him a detailed five hundred year prophecy covering all the major world events that would lead up to the coming of the Messiah. **I want to be known in heaven like that.**

DAY 205: Ezekiel 15 - 18

Shame

Never open your mouth anymore because of your shame.

There's something wrong with me. It's not that I make mistakes-- **I am a mistake.** Shame screams in your ear, creating a rift between yourself, God, and others. Shame is a killer, a ruthless mercenary that destroys everything and everyone.

Before you followed Christ, you thought like an orphan, and your tendency was self-preservation. **There was something wrong with you.** You listened to and followed the enemy of your soul, and darkness surrounded you because of it.

When the light of Christ illuminated your heart, you felt ashamed of yourself, and you were right to do so. After all, you were a broken mess who hurt yourself and others. Then Jesus made atonement for you, cleansing you of all unrighteousness, and giving you a new nature. He canceled the power of shame, and now you are free.

When you understand the power of the cross and resurrection, you must change the way you think and talk about yourself. **There is not, nor can there ever be, something wrong with you after what Jesus did for you.** It's still possible to make mistakes, and if you do, admit your guilt and make things right. But you're a child of God now, and your nature is good.

You're not broken-- you are whole. You're not a sinner-- you are a saint. You're not an orphan-- you are a child of God. You're not a victim-- you are powerful.

Never open your mouth because of shame again.

DAY 206: Ezekiel 19 - 22

Make A Wall

So I sought for a man among them who would make a wall, and stand in the gap before Me on behalf of the land, that I should not destroy it.

After all that Israel did-- idol worship, sexual immorality, oppressing the poor, and every demonic thing you could imagine-- God still cared about them. **He looked for someone, anyone, who would stand in the gap for His people, so He didn't have to destroy the land**, but there was no one.

God searched for a way to show mercy, to find a person on the earth that would use their God-given authority to make a wall to protect their people, but no one volunteered.

For some reason, many believers have adopted a false understanding of the sovereignty of God. They think circumstances on earth go well or not because God decided one way or another, but that's not how it works. **He gave authority of the planet to humans-- He accomplishes His plans by working with us.** That's why Jesus had to come as a man. He had to bind the enemy, fulfill the law, submit to God, sacrifice himself, and rise from the dead AS A HUMAN ON THE EARTH.

Our words, prayers, faith, confidence, actions, leadership, and love gives God permission to work, and He will not act without it.

Right now, in your sphere of influence, God is seeking a way to bless people. He is looking for someone to believe, lead, pray, and care so He can release the anointing, grace, revelation, power, and love that changes the world. Will you be that person?**Will you make a wall and stand in the gap for those around you?**

DAY 207: Ezekiel 23 - 26

Your Life Is Not Your Own

So I spoke to the people in the morning, and at evening my wife died; and the next morning I did as I was commanded.

Cancer. Diabetes. Heart disease. Obesity. Drug addiction. Poverty. Racism. Depression. Human trafficking. Abortion. Violence. Divorce.

The list could go on and on, but you get the point.

There are plenty of problems that still need answers, and Jesus has a target on the back of every one of them.

He is determined to bless every family, nation, language group, and ethnicity on earth.

There are plenty of resources allocated-- God has more than enough money, authority, power, love, and revelation.

There is only one thing that remains-- YOU.

The only thing standing between a problem and its solution is someone willing to partner with God to solve it. God only needs one person to believe Him and be willing to do whatever it takes.

Noah did it. So did Abraham, Ruth, Esther, David, Isaiah, Nehemiah, Daniel, Peter, and Paul. **What about you?**

There's a solution to every problem in every people group if there is one person who won't take no for an answer.

Are you in?

DAY 208: Ezekiel 27 - 30

The Original Orphan

You were perfect in your ways from the day you were created, Till iniquity was found in you.

He had it made. Perfectly designed for worship, Satan should have been the happiest creature ever created, but it wasn't enough. He didn't want to be the one offering praise; he longed to receive it.

Thus began the orphan spirit.

The devil lost his place of privilege when he decided to jump ship, and he became a master manipulator to get what he could never deserve.

The Father, in His ultimate wisdom, decided to freely give away what Satan attempted to steal-- a seat at the table. God formed man and woman in His image, calling us sons and daughters, and offered us authority on the earth.

From then on it was war, creature vs. Creator, with the devil trying to con his way into power, **but it was never a fair fight.**

Satan's legal authority is gone forever, but he still sends his minions out of spite to try to convince us that we're orphans and victims.

I don't know about you, but **I am perfectly content as a son**. I love having nothing to prove and getting to work in the family business. I enjoy living in victory and safety, never needing to earn God's favor. I like having a free will and access to all of heaven's resources.

Giving God all the honor He deserves is not a problem for me. Matter of fact, **I would much rather play a role on the winning team than be the chief victim in charge of my own life**.

DAY 209: Ezekiel 31 - 34

The Big Picture

And they shall no longer be a prey for the nations, nor shall beasts of the land devour them; but they shall dwell safely, and no one shall make them afraid.

You wake up, tired and unmotivated. You deal with immediate needs, then take care of family matters.

Maybe you get some good news, have a laugh, or enjoy a conversation with a friend, but the bills, deadlines, laundry, loneliness, or arguing kids are always lurking around the corner to jump on you if you put your guard down.

You live week to week, crisis to crisis, and it's easy to miss the big picture. If that sounds familiar, listen carefully to what I am about to say.

YOUR PERSPECTIVE DETERMINES YOUR FUTURE.

You can be happy, enjoy deep relationships, make lots of money, and change the world **if you change the way you think**, or you can write off what I'm saying and continue to think of yourself as a victim. **It's your choice.**

I know everything inside you screams that you are waiting on God to decide in your favor-- I understand, I've been there. BUT IT'S NOT TRUE!

You determine what you think, feel, desire, focus on, dream about, and do.

See yourself in the BIG PICTURE and choose to BELIEVE.

Change how you THINK and TALK yourself into HOPE.

DAY 210: Ezekiel 35 - 38

Playing A Different Game

And He said to me, "Son of man, can these bones live?"

The disciples followed Jesus around and listened to Him, but it was difficult for them to understand what He meant. The problems that concerned them never seemed to cross Jesus' mind.

It's like they were playing two different games. **The disciples were playing tee-ball while Jesus was hitting homers in the major leagues.**

Ezekiel had a similar experience. He looked out over a valley of dry bones, while God saw a vast army.

Then the Spirit came, and everything changed. Suddenly, the impossible seemed logical.

After the outpouring of the Holy Spirit, the disciples took Jesus' place in the story.

They tasted what it was like to stand at the plate in the majors-- it became normal to sleep through storms, cast out demons, and command diseases to leave.

The Spirit changes everything.

He broke the veil between heaven and earth to empower people, and He never left.

Engage your good and noble hearts with the Holy Spirit, believing that nothing is impossible, and play the game the way your created to.

DAY 211: Ezekiel 39 - 42

Face To Face

'And I will not hide My face from them anymore; for I shall have poured out My Spirit on the house of Israel,' says the Lord GOD."

Do you understand the incredible access God gave you?

The Holy Spirit dwells within you.

The One who hovered over the waters anticipating the Father's commands at creation lives in you.

You have access to the One who empowered the disciples to change the world.

God has unveiled His face and let you get to know Him.

Please, stop for a minute and ponder what is available to you.

What do you need to do that is so important that keeps you from fellowship with the Holy Spirit?

I implore you to **change the way you think.**

Don't keep going around and around the wilderness of survival when there is SO MUCH MORE!

Jesus didn't pay the ultimate price and pour out the Spirit so you could live stressed out and afraid.

You don't need five more years to "work on" whatever you are struggling with-- BELIEVE the gospel today and start living like its true.

DAY 212: Ezekiel 43 - 46

Living With God

I will dwell in their midst forever.

When you say yes to following Jesus, you are not committing to improve your life, try harder, or be a good person. **If you could do that, you wouldn't need Jesus.**

To follow Jesus, you must acknowledge that you have willingly embraced orphan thinking, repent, and allow God to give you a new nature. **Then you BELIEVE that it worked-- you are dead to sin, you're no longer a victim, and you have a good heart-- and start TALKING and ACTING as if it's already true.**

You are not "working on" becoming a good person, or "struggling" to change. You are now the temple of the Holy Spirit. You are not becoming His dwelling place; you ARE right now.

BELIEVE that it works. Identify yourself as a follower of Jesus, then talk and act like one. That means your heart is good, God talks to you, your nature is to do right, nothing is impossible, and every circumstance sets you up to succeed.

As you work WITH God to add value to others, He will take you through a process to renew your mind and restore your soul, but completing this process is NOT PROOF that you are righteous. In fact, it only happens after you know God changed your nature.

STOP "working" and "struggling" to be good, do right, and please the Father. All trying harder does is trap you in the wilderness.

You are God's house-- ACT LIKE IT.

DAY 213: Ezekiel 47 - Daniel 2

Wherever The River Goes

There will be a very great multitude of fish, because these waters go there; for they will be healed, and everything will live wherever the river goes.

Have you witnessed the power of ocean waves crashing on the shore or experienced the relaxation of floating in a pool?

Have you felt the rushing flow of the river or the excitement of being out on the lake?

I know you've had the life-giving refreshment of a cold drink.

We all love water. It's essential to all life and growth, so it's no wonder God uses a river to describe the Holy Spirit-- **He is continually moving and bringing life.**

However, sometimes we miss out because we think the river of life is a destination to visit.

You are the temple of the LIVING GOD, and the river flows from the temple, not to it.

Stop looking for life to flow to you; it doesn't work that way.

You benefit from the life-giving river of the Holy Spirit as it flows FROM you to add value to others.

You are not a victim looking for a break-- you are a source of life to everyone you know.

DAY 214: Daniel 3 - 6

Habits

Now when Daniel knew that the writing was signed, he went home. And in his upper room, with his windows open toward Jerusalem, he knelt down on his knees three times that day, and prayed and gave thanks before his God, as was his custom since early days.

Daniel knelt three times a day and prayed from the time he was a teenager until he passed away. He didn't do it to avert a crisis or celebrate a breakthrough-- it was about identity. He firmly believed, **"I'm the kind of person who honors God, no matter what."**

When he was young and unknown, he created a private ritual that he consistently did for 70 years, and he eventually became famous for his incredible wisdom and devotion to both God and the king. Daniel was repeatedly brought in to solve difficult problems, interpret troubling dreams, and give wise counsel. His gifts and loyalty got him promoted to third in command in the most powerful regime in the world, and his reputation was impeccable. **Even God bragged about him.**

All the while, Daniel was kneeling, praying, and giving thanks. **Day after day he continued, wearing out the carpet by the window in his room.** Then some jealous posers rose in power and plotted a way to catch Daniel and put him away. They got a law signed that said he would pay with his life if he prayed to his God. Under threat of death, Daniel walked home, knelt at his window, and followed his custom since childhood.

Your habits define your identity. Circumstances will rise and fall, recognition will come and go, but your customs make you who you are. Daniel went to the lion's den to protect his identity, and his relationship with God, formed by his decades of consistent prayer, allowed him to be the first person to walk out of the lion's den unscathed. **What kind of person do your daily habits say you are?**

DAY 215: Daniel 7 - 10

Power To The People

Then the kingdom and dominion, And the greatness of the kingdoms under the whole heaven, Shall be given to the people, the saints of the Most High.

The kingdom, dominion, and greatness belong to the people, the saints of the Most High. **That's you, by the way-- you're the ruling class of the earth.**

"Then why do I feel so powerless?" you may ask.

There are three possibilities: you're trying to work your way in instead of BUYING IN, you're not setting yourself up to succeed, or you don't trust your desires. Let me explain.

God gives you identity, purpose, affirmation, grace, revelation, inheritance, favor, and authority for FREE-- YOU CAN'T EARN IT. **Either you BELIEVE what God's says and get the benefits, or you miss out.**

Unless you think of yourself as the BEST IN THE WORLD, you will set yourself up with a good excuse to fail instead of giving yourself what you need to win. We all need compassion, motivation, accountability, coaching, and instruction, so why not focus on one thing you want to change, invest real money and time in yourself, and get all the help you can?

To get the kind of drive you need to add significant value to others, you MUST trust the desires God put inside you. If you don't, you won't be able to FOCUS your energy on bearing fruit, and your life will be a cycle of stress and anxiety.

Stop working to please God. BELIEVE Him, and then focus your efforts on becoming the BEST IN THE WORLD at what He called you to be.

DAY 216: Daniel 11 - Hosea 2

Shine Like Stars

Those who are wise shall shine Like the brightness of the firmament, And those who turn many to righteousness Like the stars forever and ever.

"I'm a world changer." **C'mon, just say it.**

"But I don't feel like a world changer. Can't you see, I'm barely hanging on here. I've made a ton of mistakes, and I can't even get myself to do the things I already know I'm supposed to do. How am I a world changer?"

There are three ways to approach life: quit trying and see what happens (then blame everyone else for your results), work your tail off to please God and be a good person, or BUY your way to the front of the line with FAITH.

I know you guys aren't quitters-- I'm not even going to talk about that-- so let's talk about the last two.

Jesus did all the heavy lifting to bring you into the family as full-fledged sons and daughters, all you need to do is BELIEVE. **I'm serious.** You can try your best to please God, get affirmation, earn forgiveness, do the right thing, fix your mistakes, and be a good person, but YOU WILL NEVER GET THERE! **All you're doing is labeling yourself as a slave and sentencing yourself to a life in the wilderness.**

To win in life, you can't work your way to the top-- YOU MUST BELIEVE. God said I'm a world changer, a son, forgiven, anointed, good-natured, and powerful, so I start talking and acting like it's all true. Faith is the FAST PASS to the front of the line. **You either BELIEVE what God says, or you wander around the wilderness sweating and thinking like a grasshopper.**

DAY 217: Hosea 3 - 6

A Growth Mindset

My people are destroyed for lack of knowledge.

Are we born with a fixed capacity, where you're either intelligent, creative, and out-going--or you're not--and there's not much you can do about it?

Perhaps some people hit the genetic, spiritual, or financial lottery, while others get the left-overs.

What do you think, can you improve, grow, and learn, or are you stuck with your lot in life?

Whether you adopt a fixed or a growth mindset has a significant impact on your future, and I urge you to **stay away from the lottery mindset.**

Of course, we are all born with varying capacities and in different circumstances. Our gifts, abilities, money, parents, time in history, country of origin, race, and sex are not the same.

But it's not your starting point that matters, it's your belief that you can take what you have and increase it that makes all the difference.

You can improve anything with the right mindset and hard work, and if one person can do something, so can another.

So which is it?

Are you a victim of your parents, background, authorities, circumstances, or genetics, or are you ready to believe God's word, roll up your sleeves, and get to work learning what you need to know to fulfill your destiny?

DAY 218: Hosea 7 - 10

Hit The Reset Button

Sow for yourselves righteousness; Reap in mercy; Break up your fallow ground, For it is time to seek the LORD, Till He comes and rains righteousness on you.

Renewing your mind is a process. Building a relationship with God is a lifelong pursuit. The restoration of your soul is an ongoing development. All three take time and require layers of revelation.

But those processes DO NOT make you a believer-- they happen after you are already part of the family.

Before you can ever think, feel, and act right, you must BUY INTO the identity God gave you.

Jesus came preaching, "change the way you think and believe the gospel!"

When you hear a story, message, verse, song, prophecy, or testimony that declares WHO YOU CAN BE, you either accept or reject it. In your mind, you are either an orphan or a son, a survivor or a world changer-- **you can't be both.**

YOU MUST BUY INTO THE IDENTITY GOD GIVES YOU BEFORE ANY TRANSFORMATION CAN HAPPEN.

If you CONSIDER YOURSELF a world changer, then you will begin to think, feel, and act like one, but if God speaks and you say, "that's not me," you miss out on everything He wants to do in and through your life. As soon as you hesitate, you open the door for doubt.

Hit the reset button in your mind right now, and let the renewal, restoration, and relationship begin.

DAY 219: Hosea 11 - 14

Hear The Roar

They shall walk after the LORD. He will roar like a lion. When He roars, Then His sons shall come trembling from the west.

You have the skills, the knowledge, and the heart.

You're the kind of person that goes out of your way to help others.

You willingly sacrifice to encourage your kids, friends, family, and co-workers.

You've spent years developing your relationship with God, and you would like nothing more than to please Him.

Deep inside, there is a longing to make a difference, but until now, the whisper of fear and doubt limited your impact.

In the distance, you can hear the sound of HIS voice rolling across the landscape of your mind like thunder, "You are my beloved son, in whom I am well pleased." **THE LION is roaring, and His voice shifts something inside you.**

You're a WORLD CHANGER, and you know it. You create businesses that solve critical problems. You develop people and heal broken hearts. You use your creativity to inspire the next generation. You make a living making a difference.

The ROAR of THE LION destroys the yoke of fear and doubt, releasing you from your cage. It's time to BELIEVE the words of the Father and start thinking like the WORLD CHANGER you are.

DAY 220: Amos 2 - 5

Just Say It

The Lord GOD has spoken! Who can but prophesy?

God doesn't do anything until someone on earth hears His heart, agrees with Him, and speaks it into existence.

God is a Creator, and He creates through words.

We are made in His image and have authority on the earth, so we operate the same way.

Everything good originates in the heart of God, then He broadcasts it to those who have ears to hear.

If we are listening, we tune in to what He is saying, and then the fun begins.

First, we BELIEVE what God says. **Believing is not a process, it is a decision to agree with God** made the moment we hear. Next, we change the way we THINK ABOUT OURSELVES based on what God said.

Then we change the way we TALK. We proclaim what God said about us, and begin talking to and about ourselves in a way that sets us up to succeed. Finally, we act as if everything God said is already true.

For example, if God says, "you're a good mom," then you stop looking for proof that you are, and start thinking, talking, and acting as if you're already there.

Whatever God says about you, AGREE WITH HIM AND SAY IT TOO! Stop waiting for another word, and **become the prophet for your own destiny.**

DAY 221: Amos 6 - 9

The Qualification Myth

Then Amos answered, and said to Amaziah: "I was no prophet, nor was I a son of a prophet, but I was a sheepbreeder and a tender of sycamore fruit.

What qualifies you to be a world changer?

Is it how you feel? My guess is you don't feel like a superhero 99% of the time-- no one does. Is it your education? Education is great, but it certainly does not qualify you to change the world. Is it your knowledge and experience? It sure doesn't hurt to know what you are doing, but nobody starts that way. Maybe it's your work ethic? Perhaps, but some of the hardest working people have little or no impact on the world around them. What about your family history? No way. There are many examples of people changing the world that came from difficult backgrounds.

So what qualifies someone to be a world changer? God does, of course!

He found you with zero qualifications and SPEAKS TO YOU, giving you an IDENTITY and a PURPOSE. THEN YOU BELIEVE HIM-- you submit to His calling for your life and start thinking, talking, and acting like it's true.

When you believe what He says about you, God ANOINTS you with His Spirit to do what He called you to do. Immediately, circumstances and the voice of the enemy will say THE EXACT OPPOSITE of what God said about you to test if your confidence is in anything other than GOD'S WORD.If you pass the test, you walk into your destiny FULLY QUALIFIED before you do anything to prove it.

If you can walk into a room with confidence in your identity, aware of the anointing on your life, then you are a world changer.

DAY 222: Obadiah 1 - Jonah 3

Are You Stuck In A Storm?

And he said to them, "Pick me up and throw me into the sea; then the sea will become calm for you. For I know that this great tempest is because of me."

Not all storms are created equal.

Jonah found himself in a storm because he was running from his calling. God told him to do something great, but Jonah decided it was too hard, so he hesitated. Then, when it looked like there was no other choice, Jonah decided to hop on a boat in the opposite direction. **A storm arose, not because the enemy was opposing him, but because he was going the wrong way. There were no storms on the road to Nineveh.**

The disciples found themselves in a storm a few times as well, but for other reasons. They were going in the direction Jesus told them to go, and the storm was there to teach them to use their authority.

Paul faced a storm that was not his fault at all. In fact, he was the reason everyone else survived.

Elijah even caused a storm or two.

My point is that some storms are not the opposition of the enemy, they are opportunities for you to move forward in the right direction.

Are you stuck in a storm?

Don't automatically assume that it's the enemy. **Maybe you should turn around and do the hard thing God asked you to do.**

Just a thought.

DAY 223: Jonah 4 - Micah 3

Full Of Power

But truly I am full of power by the Spirit of the LORD, and of justice and might.

It's not automatic, you know.

It's not inevitable either.

Paul prayed in Ephesians three that they would be filled with might in their inner man through His Spirit.

That means that you can show up on Sundays and NOT have might on the inside.

Jesus said that whoever believes and drinks of Him would unleash the Spirit like a river in and through them.

But it's not automatic-- **you still have to believe, and you still have to drink**.

Here's how it works: you take time to fellowship with the Holy Spirit until you get REVELATION about something, then you BELIEVE what He says and **change the way you think, feel, and act to align with it.**

If you do that on a regular basis, He will ask you to add value to others in some way. Say YES and pursue your assignment with CONFIDENCE, and you will get to taste the POWER of the Spirit flowing through you.

That's the process, and there are no shortcuts.

Start today. Take a minute right now to be aware of His presence and promises, then set your heart to partner with Him to bless someone else.

DAY 224: Micah 4 - 7

Things Are Looking Up

Now it shall come to pass in the latter days That the mountain of the LORD's house Shall be established on the top of the mountains, And shall be exalted above the hills; And peoples shall flow to it.

What do you think of when you hear the words "latter days?" Do images of nuclear war, terrible persecution, and people leaving the faith flash through your mind?

The picture Micah paints is a little different. He sees a peaceful world under the influence of Jesus in which people are seeking to follow God. Isaiah and Joel saw the same thing. They prophesied a worldwide outpouring of the Holy Spirit and the never-ending increase of Jesus' influence.

More people are coming to Christ right now than ever (100,000 a day!), the world is the most peaceful it has ever been, and poverty is at an all-time low. More miracles are taking place (hundreds raised from the dead in the last decade alone!), more people are gathering together, and the worship movement is exploding.

When Jesus is in charge, things get better, not worse.

"But what about...?" you say, "Things don't seem to be getting better around me." The culture of any family, city, or nation is directly related to the faith of the church. **You are the light of the world, so perhaps your world looks dark because your light is dim.**

Instead of whining about things, let's take a different approach. Find out what problem you are called to solve, believe that you can make a difference, and go ALL-IN until you do. **If every believer lived like that, would the world get better or worse?**

DAY 225: Nahum 1 - Habakkuk 1

Oh Lord, How Long?

O LORD, how long shall I cry, And You will not hear? Even cry out to You, "Violence!" And You will not save.

Have you ever wondered if anyone is listening up there? Things seem pretty urgent down here God; I need an answer right NOW! Um, please... Habakkuk felt like that.

Why do I keep asking if nothing is going to change? As it turns out, God was thinking a hundred moves ahead and had a perfect plan already in motion. Prayer is mysterious sometimes. **How does it work, and why?**

When you pray, start with God's promises. **There's no use asking for stuff if you are not CONFIDENT that you agree with God.**

Know your place. Prayer isn't about talking God into something that He doesn't want to do; **it's about using your position of authority on the earth to establish God's will in your sphere of influence.**

Be willing to grow. Most "delays" in answered prayer are an opportunity for us to become part of the solution.

Never take a position as the victim. God doesn't bend to manipulation, He responds to faith. When you ask for something, **ALWAYS assume that God is smarter than you, more loving than you, and way more generous than you.**

Don't quit. I guarantee that God is thinking way ahead of you, setting you up to succeed. Use your authority and relationship with Him to agree with His GOOD plan, and never, ever give up.

DAY 226: Habakkuk 2- Zephaniah 2

Write The Vision

Write the vision And make it plain on tablets, That he may run who reads it.

I cannot exaggerate the importance of this point-- **you NEED to write or speak the vision God gave you** repeatedly in front of people until it is as plain as day.

This devotion marks about two hundred and forty days in a row writing on the same subject-- identity. It all started with a stunning encounter with God, a dream inviting me to exchange my small mindedness for the anointing.

I could have continued with life as usual, but thankfully I had a mentor who challenged me to write. He said, "I want you to take the message you think you are called to and write it every day, even if no one is paying attention."

As you write or speak your core message, the fog surrounding it lifts, leaving the vision clear as day. First, it becomes clear to you, and then with repetition, you learn to explain it to others.

Every one of you has a unique identity and purpose, with a core message attached to it. **Don't make the mistake of thinking that the passage of time alone will fulfill the dream God put inside you** -- YOU MUST PUBLISH CONTENT ON YOUR TOPIC CONSISTENTLY FOR A LONG TIME.

Do it for yourself at first, then do it to serve those who are paying attention. Eventually, you'll do it to attract followers so that you can help them get real results, and if you do it well, a steady stream of income. Once the vision God gave you is crystal clear, it will change your life and those around you.

DAY 227: Zephaniah 3 - Zechariah 1

The Craftsmen Revival

Then the LORD showed me four craftsmen.

I dream of a million revivalists making the world a better place.

But these revivalists are different than anything the world has ever seen. Most of them are not on staff at a church or missions organization-- they're **creative entrepreneurs** attacking a problem with a mandate from God.

Sure, they love God and are a part of a body of believers, but they are so much more than that. They have a solid foundation in the essentials-- health, money, and relationships-- but that's not the goal; it's just the starting line.

They are under orders from heaven to add value to the world, not hide in a corner in fear.

These revivalists are writers, singers, musicians, speakers, artists, coaches, business owners, and leaders. They create and sell products and services that change the world, and they make a good living doing it.

The gifts of the Holy Spirit operate fully in their lives, and they are not ashamed to admit it.

They are not poor, uneducated, or scared; they are sons and daughters of the living God.

They are crystal clear about their identity, confident, motivated, emotionally and relationally whole, focused, and doggedly persistent.

ARE YOU A CRAFTSMEN REVIVALIST?

DAY 228: Zechariah 2 - 5

The Day Of Small Beginnings

Who are you, O great mountain? Before Zerubbabel you shall become a plain! And he shall bring forth the capstone With shouts of "Grace, grace to it!

Just do it!

Run with the vision God gave you, and don't look back.

So what if people don't believe in you; that's never stopped a World Changer before.

Believe in yourself.

Does it matter if you don't have a million dollar idea yet?

Listen to what God already spoke to you, and start growing.

Who cares if it makes you uncomfortable or takes a long time-- **what else is there to do? Either you're going to hang out in the wilderness for the rest of your life, or you're going to face your fears and go for it.**

It may be small and unimpressive right now, but everything starts that way. Every fruit tree starts as a seed planted below the surface. No one but you even knows the seed is there, but that doesn't discount its importance.

Your dreams will grow as big as you do, so keep growing!

If you wait until next week or next month or next year, you will never do it.

Do it NOW!

DAY 229: Zechariah 6 - 9

Prisoners Of Hope

Return to the stronghold, You prisoners of hope. Even today I declare That I will restore double to you.

You go to sleep telling yourself that tomorrow will be better than today. It's not a lie-- you genuinely believe it. You expect good things to happen in and through your life. Then you wake up, sluggish to get the day started, but grateful to be alive. Slowly the day unfolds. You do your job, pay your bills, put out fires, and deal with people.

Somewhere during the day you give up on it and turn your expectations to the next one. Tomorrow will be better. This nagging loneliness will go away. That person or problem will leave you alone. You'll make progress on that project. You can't give up on hope; sometime, somewhere, good things are going to happen, right?

Hope is hard sometimes. On the one hand, hope is a stronghold you retreat into to protect you from fear, depression, and bitterness. **But other times, hope feels like a prison. Expecting good in the future makes you feel like a victim today.** So what do you do? You can't give up, but the waiting is driving you crazy.

I don't have all the answers, but I want to share something that has helped me a lot-- I call it **active hope.** EVERY SINGLE DAY, DON'T JUST GET YOUR HOPES UP-- DO SOMETHING THAT MOVES YOU CLOSER TO THE THING YOU WANT.

Learn something, make a call, set up a meeting, do a workout, go on a date, say no to a brownie, read a chapter, pay down your credit card debt-- **do something, anything, that helps you physically agree with what you are hoping for.**

DAY 230: Zechariah 10 - 13

The Big Buy In

In that day a fountain shall be opened for the house of David and for the inhabitants of Jerusalem, for sin and for uncleanness.

When did being a Christian get so hard? We live stressed out all the time, and trying to get God to do something we want feels like pulling teeth. We beg and plead for revival, but expect that it is going to take forever if it ever comes at all. We're always working on something, but never seem to make progress. Sure, there are moments in worship we enjoy, and the occasional testimony or breakthrough that keeps us going, but then it's back to the grind. Does it have to be this way?

Although this is a typical experience for many believers, what I described above is NOT the Christian life. The truth is, the life of a believer is the best life and BY FAR the easiest. Then **why does it feel so hard for most people?** It's simple-- **fear of the unknown causes us to hold on to CONTROL**, which in turn requires us to work for things that are free. We work so hard to be good and keep "believing" for God to help us out, but nothing changes. We're stressed out all the time because we never seem to live up to the standard, so we back off a little and take comfort in "grace" and "mercy," and the occasional piece of cherry pie (which makes us feel guilty and starts the cycle all over again.)

It does not have to be like this you know. If a girl falls madly in love with a handsome, wealthy, and kind young man, is it hard for her to spend time with him? It is the same with Jesus. **The entire Christian life is about the BIG BUY IN.** We talk to God, listen to Him, and fall in love. It's the most natural thing in the world because we enjoy it. **It's only hard for those who hang on to control because of fear.** Stop working for the things that are free, and enjoy Jesus. His love is SO MUCH BETTER than staying in control.

DAY 231: Zechariah 14 - Malachi 3

His Name Shall Be Great

For from the rising of the sun, even to its going down, My name shall be great among the Gentiles; In every place incense shall be offered to My name, And a pure offering; For My name shall be great among the nations.

Did you know that you are the fulfillment of prophecy?

Not only that, you are the fulfillment of God's dream for the earth.

All along He intended that His name would be great from the rising of the sun to it's going down, and you are making that happen.

When we offer lives of devotion and wholehearted worship, we add greatness to His name among our families, cities, and nations.

When we tell someone else about Jesus, sacrifice to obey Him, or love His people well, we extend His kingdom around the globe.

Don't let months and years go by unaware of your role on the earth.

No believer is here to survive-- we exist to advance the kingdom of God.

Make His name great by offering your life in extravagant worship, love, sacrifice, obedience, and devotion.

Live to love.

Live as if the reputation of Jesus depended solely on your example, and stay aware of your place in the bigger story.

DAY 232: Malachi 4 - Matthew 3

The Transition

And suddenly a voice came from heaven, saying, "This is My beloved Son, in whom I am well pleased."

For years you lived a relatively normal life, but something is shifting inside you.

It's like a grand old clock is chiming in your soul, declaring that it's time. Time for what, you are not sure, but SOMETHING is happening.

You want more. Your restless heart begins to search for answers, and before long, you find yourself at a place of decision.

With no assurances about what's next, you head down to the river of surrender.

Before God and everyone, you decide to GO ALL IN, giving yourself wholly to the King and His kingdom.

You long for intimacy, influence, impact, and increase, so you ready yourself to take the plunge.

You dive in, surrendering everything to the will of God, then emerge to the bright light of revelation.

"You are my beloved son, in whom I am well pleased," rings in your ears, a vote of confidence from the Father.

The Spirit of God comes upon you, empowering you for the task ahead.

Normal is over. Time to change the world.

DAY 234: Matthew 4 - 7

If You Are The Son Of God

Now when the tempter came to Him, he said, "If You are the Son of God..."

IF. **All the enemy needs to derail your future is one IF.**

Certain things ONLY exist because God said so, you can't prove them.

God forgave you. The Father accepted you, adopting you into His family. He gave you significance, identity, and purpose. The Holy spirit anointed you. God called you to change the world. **You can't do those things for yourself, neither can you prove that they are true.**

The WORDS OF GOD create the core beliefs that lay the foundation for your future success; there is no other evidence. Therefore, for you to become who God made you to be, you MUST start with FAITH in what He says about you.

God will speak to you-- through the Bible, impressions, dreams, prophecies, sermons, teachings, songs, unusual circumstances, visions, etc...-- and then you must believe Him. Don't look around your life or heart for proof that He is right. **God's words create reality; they do not require proof.**

You believe what God says about you with CERTAINTY, and live as if everything He says is accurate in the present moment.

You can't "work on" becoming a son, receiving a calling, feeling forgiven-- those things are only valid because God said so.

You either BELIEVE it and begin thinking, talking, and acting like it's already true, or Satan will bully you into a life of survival in the wilderness.

DAY 235: Matthew 8 - 11

Moved With Compassion

But when He saw the multitudes, He was moved with compassion for them, because they were weary and scattered, like sheep having no shepherd.

The foundation of all lasting change is compassion. Think about that statement for a moment, then consider all the other techniques we use to motivate ourselves. We tend to bully through fear or manipulate with the promise of reward, and those work for a while, but the motivation wanes with time, and we end up back where we started.

Instead of trying to force change, try leading yourself with genuine compassion. Take the time to acknowledge the real and immediate problems you face. Don't sugar coat them-- let reality set in. Then allow yourself to feel genuine compassion by asking a couple of questions. How did I end up here? What do I need to change?

We all require inspiration, belief, examples, instruction, leadership, accountability, resources, and community to create new habits. **Without compassion, we tend to look for a reason to fail instead of setting ourselves to succeed.**

Compassion says that your heart is good, your problems are real, and you can do it with the right help. It pushes us to seek the Lord for real solutions and to implement the answers we get in prayer.

Take a break from bullying yourself long enough to assess your situation. Have you been struggling with the same area for months and years? **Stop the cycle of manipulation that leads to half-hearted action that produces shame and eventually makes you quit.**

Stop looking for excuses to fail, and let compassion move you.

DAY 236: Matthew 12 - 15

Good Soil

But others fell on good ground and yielded a crop: some a hundredfold, some sixty, some thirty.

If you get this, you get everything, so listen up.

God is the initiator of all good things. He SPEAKS to us IDEAS from heaven, each of which contains the potential to change the world. Everything He says is packed with wisdom and grace and is ready to grow and bear fruit.

BUT MOST OF WHAT GOD SAYS DOES NOT BEAR FRUIT.

God's words wither not because the ideas are bad or the circumstances are wrong; **they wilt because of the condition of the heart that receives them.** You must understand and accept responsibility for your mind, emotions, and desires before anything will change in your life.

For your heart to be GOOD SOIL that grows God ideas into loving relationships, influence, miracles, and resources, you must believe the following:

I am a world changer! I have a unique identity and purpose that is critical to the building of the kingdom, and I can hear from God. My life is my responsibility, my heart is GOOD, and I am no longer a victim or an orphan!

It's my job to cultivate confidence, motivation, and wholeness-- my happiness is up to me. I am not waiting on God, and the enemy will not steal from me. **I am supposed to live a life of abundance!**

DAY 237: Matthew 16 - 19

Nothing Is Impossible

If you have faith as a mustard seed, you will say to this mountain, 'Move from here to there,' and it will move; and nothing will be impossible for you.

Ever faced an impossible situation? How did you feel?

If you are like the disciples in Matthew 17, you felt helpless and frustrated. They faced a difficult and emotional problem, and they tried their best to solve it, but nothing worked. Jesus came and cleaned up their mess, but rebuked them in the process. Later, they got Jesus alone and asked Him what they did wrong. "Why could you solve the problem, and we got stuck?"

"**Because of your unbelief**," He said, and went on to explain the problem in more detail. Do you remember how I taught you to cultivate your heart into good soil so you can receive my words and grow them? Well, you're doing an excellent job hearing my words and producing fruit in your own life, but when you get into a situation where you are the sower, you freeze up. **You know how to receive from God, but you don't understand how to be Jesus in the story.**

If you have faith as a mustard seed, Jesus went on to explain, then you can speak to impossibilities, and they will move. The mustard seed is tiny, but it sprouts immediately and grows into the largest of all the herbs. **You need to switch gears, with the help of some prayer and fasting, from receiver to sower.**

You must believe that you can speak to problems and release powerful solutions. If you think like that, the way I do, **nothing will be impossible** for you.

DAY 238: Matthew 20 - 23

Greatness

Whoever desires to become great among you, let him be your servant.

Human nature longs to win the lottery.

We wish for the big promotion or raise that does not carry any extra responsibility.

We daydream of the handsome and wealthy husband riding in and rescuing us.

We imagine what we would do if we invested a few dollars and it magically turned into millions.

We wonder what it would be like to be born into a wealthy family or to grow up with natural beauty, athletic ability, or a genius IQ.

We call this wishful thinking HOPE.

Oh God, let me keep thinking, feeling, and acting the same way but get a much better result.

I want a great marriage, family, career, business, bank account, impact, or whatever, but I want you to decide and give it to me.

But the kingdom doesn't work that way.

Jesus loves His people to desire greatness, but it doesn't come through the divine lottery system. **Greatness is reserved for those who serve the most people at the deepest level.**

DAY 239: Matthew 24 - 27

Survival Sucks

For to everyone who has, more will be given, and he will have abundance; but from him who does not have, even what he has will be taken away.

"You wicked and lazy servant." Ouch-- I sure don't want to hear that from Jesus. What did the guy in the parable do to deserve such harsh criticism?

He survived. He paid his bills, maintained his house, and showed up for his job. He took the identity, revelation, gifts, anointing, opportunities, and relationships he received and kept them safe. From the outside, he looked faithful, but on the inside, fear ruled his life.

"I didn't know what to pursue, so I played it safe," he said, but Jesus could not believe His ears. "I didn't come from heaven, turn the world upside down, sacrifice my life, rise from the dead, and pour out My Spirit so you could play it safe!"

If you follow the King, you live in a kingdom. You rule and conquer, and you increase continually. **If you are a disciple of the World Changer, you become a world changer**-- no believers hide in fear.

Lift your vision higher! Learn to take your five talents and turn them into ten, and refuse to settle for "faithful."

If you are not increasing your influence, love, miracles, and resources, it's time to re-evaluate.

Enough hiding in fear, holding on until the Lord comes.

Let's change the world.

DAY 240: Matthew 28 - Mark 3

Follow Me!

He went up on the mountain and called to Him those He Himself wanted. And they came to Him.

Jesus wants to talk to you for a minute.

"Will you meet with me for a second, I have something I want to ask you? I have a plan. **I'm taking over the world, and I want you to help me.**"

"I am building a kingdom, and my agenda is to empower every person on the planet. **I want to eradicate poverty, disease, anxiety, depression, racism, violence, fear, addiction, and divorce-- will you help me?"**

"My vision is an earth covered with worship, revelation, inspiration, and the anointing of My Spirit, where every person has a loving family, health and fitness, nutritious food, safety, identity and purpose, and meaningful work."

"I need you to **stop worrying about all the stuff others fret about and GO ALL IN.** If you believe me, I'll give you everything you need to succeed. I'll provide forgiveness, acceptance, community, inspiration, revelation, grace, authority, anointing, gifts-- anything you need, it's yours-- and I'll be right there with you every step of the way."

"Let's make a deal. You stop worrying about the things you need to survive and let me take care of that. Instead, fellowship with my Spirit every day, and begin asking, '**How can we take over the world today?'"**

"Let go of your insecurities and fears, and say yes to starting businesses, going on camera, leading organizations, creating products, loving the unlovable, training the next generation, and solving problems. **Are you in?"**

DAY 241: Mark 4 - 7

Accept It

These are the ones sown on good ground, those who hear the word, accept it, and bear fruit.

I know you heard from God; He said something about WHO YOU ARE that got you excited. Think about it-- the One whose words created everything spoke to you too. **If that is true, then why aren't you changing the world right now?**

There are three possible reasons:

1. When God spoke to you, you heard what He said through the lens of insecurity, discounted it, and the enemy stole the word from you.
2. When you heard what He said, you got excited and began to pursue it, but the unresolved pain from broken relationships stunted its growth. Grief, unforgiveness, betrayal, fear, depression, or anger caused your excitement to wither, and what God said dried up under the heat of those overwhelming emotions.
3. When God spoke to you, His word immediately started to prosper inside you. However, your desire waned as financial pressure, busyness, and stress siphoned your focus away.

Let's be honest. You're not waiting on God, fighting the devil, or suffering oppression from others. **If we're not growing God's ideas into loving relationships, increased influence, abundant resources, and miracles, it's because we're scared, hurt, or stressed out.** BUT THAT CAN CHANGE RIGHT NOW!

The condition of your heart doesn't change because you "work on it" for a long time. **It changes by BELIEVING what God says about you, ACCEPTING it, and LIVING as if it is already true.**

DAY 242: Mark 8 - 11

What's The Problem?

I have compassion on the multitude, because they have now continued with Me three days and have nothing to eat.

Jesus is the ultimate problem solver. He will tackle anything no matter how big or small, and when you follow Him, it's only a matter of time until He starts recruiting you to help. So my question is, **what is the problem Jesus is recruiting you to help solve?** If you read Psalm 72, you will see Jesus' vision for the planet. His agenda includes:

Salvation-- He desires every person to feel forgiven, clean, and whole.
Adoption-- He wants each person to reconnect with the Father, and to understand their unique identity and purpose.
Empowering-- He longs to fill people with His Spirit, giving them access to revelation, power, and love.
Freedom-- Jesus wants to deliver every person from depression, anxiety, addiction, and torment.
Health-- He desires all to live healthy physically, mentally, and emotionally.
Nutrition-- He wants everyone to have enough nutritious food and clean water.
Safety-- He desires a world without war or violence.
Justice-- He longs to build communities without prejudice, racism, oppression, or fear.
Righteousness-- Jesus is the King of doing things the right way.
Excellence-- He knows how to do education, government, and business.
Abundance-- He wants each person to do meaningful work and have more than enough resources.
Family-- He desires to eradicate loneliness and promote genuine love.
Worship-- Jesus is all about honoring the Father with the extravagant worship He deserves.
So, what problem is He talking to you about?

DAY 243: Mark 12 - 15

What Now?

Peter called to mind the word that Jesus had said to him, "Before the rooster crows twice, you will deny Me three times." And when he thought about it, he wept.

You just blew it big time. The thing you thought you would never do, even promised to do the opposite, you did. God trusted you with an assignment, and you let Him down. You were supposed to be the leader, the person others could count on, and **now you're blubbering with your head buried in your hands.** WHAT NOW?

What do you do when fear overwhelms your faith, and you do exactly the opposite of what you wanted to? **You cry.**

The worst thing you can do in those moments is to pick yourself up and move on-- you need to grieve. It's not about giving in to shame and having a pity party; **it's about being honest with yourself.** Before you can recover and grow into the person you need to be, you MUST tell yourself the truth, and allow the tears to flow.

If you don't grieve your mistakes and failures, admitting the cold, hard facts, then you can't move on. **If you make up a story to temporarily cheer yourself up, you will trap those emotions and regrets inside to resurface later.**

THE FOUNDATION OF ALL HAPPINESS AND WHOLENESS IS HONESTY.

Jesus can restore, disciple, and empower you for the assignment ahead if you cry when you make a mistake. Don't let busyness keep you from grieving, repentance, and being honest with yourself.

DAY 244: Mark 16 - Luke 3

Greatness Is Going First

"He will also go before Him in the spirit and power of Elijah, 'to turn the hearts of the fathers to the children,' and the disobedient to the wisdom of the just, to make ready a people prepared for the Lord."

Do you ever feel like you're always the first one out of all your friends and family to do something?

Maybe you're the first one to finish college, start a business, write a book, record an album, or lose weight.

Perhaps the message God called you to trumpet is something no one around you has heard before.

Being the pioneer clearing the land for the first time can be lonely, but I want you to know you are not alone.

I understand how you feel.

MOST OF THE TIME BEING GREAT MEANS GOING FIRST.

Don't make the mistake I did for many years. I was willing to go before others, but I was not ready to gather and lead them all the way to the results they needed.

If you are the forerunner in your sphere of influence, remember, you are not alone. God is raising up people like you all over the earth.

Say yes to selling, gathering, leadership, and organizing. **Don't show others what to do and then leave them to figure it out for themselves-- guide them to success.**

DAY 245: Luke 4 - 7

I'm The One

And He began to say to them, "Today this Scripture is fulfilled in your hearing."

At some point, God will call your name, asking you to help solve a problem. If you believe Him and respond, the Father will anoint you with His Spirit, empowering you with the revelation and power you need to do the task.

Then it's time for the test. The enemy and your circumstances will scream the exact opposite of what God said about you, to see if you believe God's words just because He spoke them.

When you pass the test, you will walk out of survival and begin doing what you are called to do. People will begin to respond, and you will start solving the problems you are anointed to solve.

Then something strange will happen. You'll be excited about what you're learning and the results you're getting, but **the people that knew you while you were still a survivor will be skeptical.** Many of them will not be able to get over the fact that you grew up with them or used to be in the same place they are now.

What are you going to do? Are you going to tone it down, back off, and fit in with your friends and family? **Nope.**

You are going to stand up and say, **"I am the answer to your prayers and the one you've been waiting for-- God anointed me to solve the problem you are struggling with."** Most of them won't respond, but things will shift inside you.

You are no longer the survivor they remember; **you are the anointed of the Lord.**

DAY 246: Luke 8 - 11

How You Hear

"Therefore take heed how you hear. For whoever has, to him more will be given; and whoever does not have, even what he seems to have will be taken from him."

"I need to hear from God," we say. Whenever there is a crisis to avert, a problem to solve, a decision to make, or a fear to overcome, we long for God to speak to us. We know that if God talks, somehow things will work out, and we're right. The voice of God is the most potent force in the universe, initiating and creating every good thing.

We care deeply about what God says and how He says it, tuning our ears to the impression, sermon, song, dream, prophecy, or unusual coincidence that we hope will guide us. **But we often ignore how we hear.** I don't mean the way we hear from God-- **I am referring to the perspective through which we filter His words.**

You see, everything God says, even the slightest impression, has the potential to grow into a fruitful idea that changes the world. However, it is not what **God says that matters most; it is the condition of the listener's heart that counts.** The way we think determines the fruitfulness of our lives.

We often make negative assumptions like: the world is getting worse, Christianity is on the decline, I am just not good at that, my heart is deceitful, I can't trust my desires, someone else is to blame, I can't control how I feel, I don't have the time, money, or energy, and I don't know how. The list could go on and on, but you get the point.

When we look at the world, others, and ourselves through a lens of fear and doubt, THE IDEAS GOD GIVES US DON'T GROW. For things to change in your life, THE WAY YOU THINK MUST CHANGE FIRST.

DAY 247: Luke 12 - 15

Your Level Of Service

When an innumerable multitude of people had gathered together, so that they trampled one another...

How much personal development do you need to survive? **None.**

If you don't see yourself as the kind of person who serves others, you won't even try to cultivate a good and noble heart.

YOUR LEVEL OF PERSONAL DEVELOPMENT CORRELATES DIRECTLY TO THE LEVEL YOU BELIEVE YOU ARE CALLED TO SERVE OTHERS.

If you're only going to feed yourself, why start farming?

You won't-- you'll go to the store and buy only the food you need.

If you want to feed a family all year round, you cultivate a garden. An acre of ground is plenty to provide for even the largest of families.

But if you believe you are called to serve thousands, then you MUST develop yourself on a larger scale.

Your ability to communicate, lead, forgive, sell, delegate, learn, think, focus, and control your emotions must flourish if you desire to serve the masses.

If you want to grow, focus on your IDENTITY.

Find out what God wants you to do and who He called you to serve, then dedicate your imagination, belief, focus, and desire to SERVING at your maximum capacity.

DAY 248: Luke 16 - 19

Becoming Profitable

"So likewise you, when you have done all those things which you are commanded, say, 'We are unprofitable servants. We have done what was our duty to do.' "

Getting into the Kingdom of Heaven is free. Well, not exactly-- it's the most expensive thing ever, costing Jesus His life-- **but it's free to you.** All you have to do is humble yourself, admit that Jesus is the only way, and BELIEVE.

Believe that the Father created all things, and He wants you as His own. Believe that Jesus died for you, rose again, and ascended into heaven, preparing the way for you to connect with the Father.

Believe that the Spirit of God dwells inside you, empowering you with revelation, grace, and the anointing. Believe that every word God speaks about you is true, and receive those words with confidence, wholeness, and focus.

So, you're in God's kingdom, now what? You got in for free, but God made a BIG investment to set you free, adopt you, and empower you to change the world, and **He expects a return on His investment.**

God is not running a charity-- He desires those who have freely received to give back, making the world a better place.

He expects you to believe every word He says, no exceptions. He requires you to take the gifts He gave and steward them well. He demands obedience when He tells you to do something, every time.

God wants you to long for more, to become addicted to the anointing and maximize your influence to help others.

DAY 249: Luke 20 - 23

Your Life Matters

I bestow upon you a kingdom, just as My Father bestowed one upon Me.

As the Father gave Jesus an assignment and the authority to fulfill it, Jesus is calling you.

You don't need to worry about the resources necessary to do your job-- God will take of that. **You must get clear answers to some vital questions.**

Who am I called by God to serve? What problems am I supposed to solve? What sphere of influence am I called to bless? How do I access the anointing and resources God made available for me to do my job? Am I willing to become a servant leader, an example for others to gather around? Will I persevere through opposition and give my life to fulfill God's plan?

If you get crystal clear about your IDENTITY, or WHO GOD CALLED YOU TO BE, then confidence, motivation, happiness, and focus will follow.

You are called to lead, sell, serve, solve problems, and add value-- we all are-- and God will reward you for your service.

Jesus is a real King, ruling a legitimate Kingdom, with the expressed purpose of taking over the world.

But it's the way He does it that separates Him from every other King. Jesus gets down in the dirt with His people, empowering them to make a meaningful contribution to the world around them.

Now He is calling you to do the same.

DAY 250: Luke 24 - John 3

Come And See

They said to Him, "Rabbi" (which is to say, when translated, Teacher), "where are You staying?" He said to them, "Come and see."

How do you take a bunch of ordinary guys and turn them into world changers? First of all, let's get one thing straight-- **ordinary people are the only kind of people there are.** If you think successful people were born with something special that you don't have, your dead wrong. No one is inherently better than anyone else.

So how do you turn average people into world changers? It starts with a basic understanding of how God created us. When the Father designed humans, **He hard-wired us to live by faith.** God talks, revealing the incredible story of why we are here, how to prosper, and what the future holds, and we BELIEVE what He says.

When we see where we fit in the story, that forms our IDENTITY, which is the foundation of all we do. So, to answer the original question-- **you turn ordinary people into world changers by SELLING them on their place in the story**, our redemption through Jesus, and the advancing Kingdom of God. When we IDENTIFY where we fit in the story, our confidence, motivation, happiness, and focus develop, and we are ready to learn HOW.

Notice how Jesus called the disciples. He didn't teach them how to have a better marriage or convince them to show up at the synagogue more often.

He SOLD them, with John's help, on the fact that He was the Messiah, the One initiating the Kingdom of God. Then He SOLD them on where they fit in the story. **Before they ever heard a word of teaching, they were ALL IN, eager to listen to every word Jesus said.**

DAY 251: John 4 - 7

Kingdom Logic

You search the Scriptures, for in them you think you have eternal life;·and these are they which testify of Me.

If you follow Jesus as your Lord and Savior, you have to believe His teachings. If you receive Jesus' words as truth, you must understand that you are adopted, forgiven, accepted, and empowered by the Spirit of God.

If you know that you are a child of God, then it stands to reason that you are a king and a priest with access to heaven and authority over the enemy. Therefore, **if you are a believer in Jesus, you are a WORLD CHANGER**-- it is impossible to hear His words and stay an orphan or a victim.

But I feel like a victim! I'm barely surviving out here, struggling with my health, relationships, finances, and inner life-- how can you say I am a world changer? Let me share an incredible truth with you (it could be the most valuable thing you've ever heard!) **Are you ready?**

IDENTITY + INTIMACY = IMPACT

Get a clear understanding of your identity (where you fit in the story, what Jesus did for you, and who you are called to be.) Add regular time with Jesus loving Him and paying attention to what He says.

And you will start to bear fruit. Your impact (the love, miracles, influence, and resources you produce) will increase and add value to the people around you.

Then you can multiply that impact by learning how to sell, lead, and cooperate with the Holy Spirit. **Ready to change the world?**

DAY 252: John 8 - 11

Confident Humility

"I am the light of the world. He who follows Me shall not walk in darkness, but have the light of life."

Jesus looked them straight in the eyes and said, **"I am the light of the world."** In other words, "I am the answer to your problems. Follow me, and you will end up in the right place."

However, Jesus gladly admitted that without the Father's blessing and assistance, He could do nothing.

That is the position you find yourself in today.

Jesus commissioned you, declaring that you are the light of the world. He also said that as the Father sent Him, He is sending you.

You are Jesus in the story.

Can you look someone in the eyes and tell them to follow you into health, forgiveness, happiness, peace, love, and abundance?

Do you think, feel, and act like the light of the world? **If not, you need to grow your confidence.**

At the same time, never forget who your source is. Without the revelation, love, acceptance, grace, mercy, and power you receive from heaven, you have nothing to offer.

You must walk in BOTH extreme confidence and humility. There is a portion of humanity waiting for you to shine bright so they can follow you into the light.

DAY 253: John 12 - 15

Assume God Is With You

I am the vine, you are the branches. He who abides in Me, and I in him, bears much fruit; for without Me you can do nothing.

"Without Me, you can do nothing." I've heard that statement Jesus told His disciples in John 15 most of my life, and I was led to believe I was missing some "special" relationship with God that only the "anointed" people possessed.

But that's not what Jesus meant. He illustrated to His disciples THE MODEL to follow-- the relationship He had with the Father.

Jesus taught them that **you need two things to bear fruit: identity and intimacy.**

You must BELIEVE that God is GOOD, you are GOOD, and the purpose for which God created you is GOOD. Then you live aware of God's presence by talking to Him, listening to Him, and loving Him.

With those things in place, you will bear fruit-- it really is that simple.

If you want to bear more fruit, you either **improve your identity** (think about yourself better), or **increase your intimacy** (live more aware of His presence), or both.

It is true that without Him you can do nothing, but that is not the point-- Jesus is pulling back the curtain and revealing how to bear fruit through abiding in His love.

ALWAYS ASSUME THAT JESUS IS WITH YOU, and you will produce genuine love, abundant resources, miracles, and increasing influence.

DAY 254: John 16 - 19

Father, Glorify Your Son

Father, the hour has come. Glorify Your Son, that Your Son also may glorify You.

Father, make me famous.

Set me up as an example for many people to follow.

Glorify me.

Let light, hope, and revelation stream from me to the world around, guiding them to you.

I am your son, and I want to be just like you.

Make me famous, an example, a leader, and a voice for my generation.

Look no farther-- let Your favor, love, and power rest on me, and use me however you desire.

You said I am the light of the world, and I believe you.

Don't hide me any longer.

I refuse to allow insecurity and fear to restrict Your anointing on my life.

Speak to me, and I will joyfully receive Your words and grow them with confidence.

Enough of the small stuff-- let's do something **BIG** together.

DAY 255: John 20 - Acts 2

I Also Send You

So Jesus said to them again, "Peace to you! As the Father has sent Me, I also send you."

"As the Father sent Me, I also send you." Let that statement resonate through your heart and mind for a minute.

The Father chose Jesus before the foundation of the world to change the course of history and redeem humanity. He sent Jesus with ALL the authority of Heaven to gather a group of people to Himself, demonstrate the heart of the Father, and teach them about the Kingdom.

The Father asked Jesus to draw huge crowds, become a public figure, offer a new opportunity, give His life for His people, and empower them to pick up where He left off.

"As the Father sent Me..." You are sent with the same authority and agenda, to bring Heaven to earth and change the course of history.

"I also send you..."

YOU ARE NOT ON THIS PLANET TO SURVIVE!

You are a voice, a leader, and a perfect reflection of the One who sent you.

BELIEVE what I am saying to you right now and GO ALL IN. When you BUY INTO the calling on your life, your mind, heart, mouth, and actions will follow.

QUIT looking for evidence God's words about you are accurate-- **let His voice create the reality INSIDE you**, and it will eventually manifest to the world.

DAY 256: Acts 3 - 6

Boldness

Now when they saw the boldness of Peter and John, and perceived that they were uneducated and untrained men, they marveled. And they realized that they had been with Jesus.

How many ideas have you had in the last year?

How many encounters with God have you experienced?

What about all those times in worship where you felt His presence or the light bulb moments while studying the Scriptures?

Remember all the dreams, desires, and impressions God gave you?

You know the difference between those who are changing the world and those who are not?

The first group thinks of themselves as world changers-- therefore, they consider every idea, dream, desire, or encounter to be a seed they can grow into something awesome.

They change the way they think, feel, and talk based on what God says, and they take immediate ACTION to turn His words into fruit.

Because they BELIEVE a whisper from God can change history, and they BUY INTO their identity as a world changer, they have BOLDNESS to act.

"God, give me MORE BOLDNESS! Give me the confidence to speak, sell, lead, recruit, create, and pray crazy big prayers!"

Change the way you think about yourself, and you will change the world.

DAY 257: Acts 7 - 10

Doubting Nothing

While Peter thought about the vision, the Spirit said to him, "Behold, three men are seeking you. "Arise therefore, go down and go with them, doubting nothing; for I have sent them."

What is the difference between you and Peter? He was a regular guy with a normal job, trying to do the best he could for his family-- and then he met Jesus.

Jesus was fascinating and mysterious, and **Peter left behind survival in pursuit of impact.** In one day everything changed, but Peter was still Peter.

With his big mouth and limited patience, Peter experienced some incredible moments (he walked on water!), and some disappointing setbacks (he rebuked and denied Jesus.)

Then he quit. He decided he was not good enough to be what Jesus wanted him to be, so he went back to survival. Jesus, however, can be very persuasive. He restored Peter, recommissioned him, and empowered him with the Holy Spirit.

Fast forward a few years, Peter is sitting on a roof praying and worshiping. The Holy Spirit shows him a vision, instructing him to go against everything he was taught growing up.

Then he hears from God-- the same Holy Spirit who talks to us gives him an impression just like he does right now. **"Get up and act, doubting nothing."** So Peter, going way outside his comfort zone, took action.

Those who change the world TAKE ACTION immediately when God speaks to them.

DAY 258: Acts 11 - 14

Sent By The Spirit

The Holy Spirit said, "Now separate to Me Barnabas and Saul for the work to which I have called them."

About one out of a hundred believers end up on staff at a church, non-profit, or missions organization. **But what about the rest of us? What are we supposed to do with our lives?**

The checklist for a typical believer not "called to the ministry" looks something like this:

Go to church as often as possible. Give money to the church (bonus points for giving 10%!) Be nice. Tell a few people a year about Jesus, or invite them to church. Spend the other 95% of your week in survival mode trying to pay bills, deal with problems, and take care of your family.

I don't know about you, but that sounds boring. I think every believer is "called" to advance the Kingdom of God, whether they are on staff at a church or not, and I think we should do it for a living. **There should be no survivors, victims, or orphans among us.**

The agenda of King should be the agenda of every person in the Kingdom:

Connect every person on earth with the Father. Improve physical, mental, and emotional health. Destroy the work of the enemy, including addiction, divorce, and torment. Keep people free and safe. Grow and distribute an abundance of nutritious food. Create wealth and solve problems. Care for and train the next generation. Cover the earth with worship and revelation. Increase beauty and joy in the world.

What are you being sent by the Spirit to do?

DAY 259: Acts 15 - 18

Changing The World

These who have turned the world upside down have come here too.

Am I crazy?

Why am I so driven to make an impact, do something meaningful, and change the world?

I look around and wonder, what does it feel like to be normal? Everyone else is dropping their kids off at school, going to work, and heading home. Maybe they want more, but I can't tell.

There is something inside me that screams for greatness, and it scares me.

What's wrong with me? I feel irresponsible. I feel embarrassed.

The craving to learn and grow consumes me, and when I can't figure something out, I can't sleep.

I love my family, and I want to provide security for them, but it's hard--really hard.

I know I'm almost there, just one idea away from a breakthrough.

My biggest fear is that the world will be the same with or without me, that I won't make a difference.

I was born to turn the world upside down, I know it.

I just know it.

DAY 260: Acts 19 - 22

Baptized In Fire

He said to them, "Did you receive the Holy Spirit when you believed?"

"Into what then were you baptized?" Paul asked. **That's a good question.**

To be baptized into something is to STOP identifying yourself one way, and START identifying yourself another. **It's all about BUY IN.**

A leader stands up and shouts, "Follow me to get these results!" and you BELIEVE what they say and IDENTIFY as their disciple. Baptism is the public demonstration that you're ALL IN.

John baptized people into repentance, preparing their hearts and minds for Jesus. When you BELIEVED what John said, you demonstrated it by getting dunked in the river.

After you identify yourself as humble, repentant, and ready for a new life, the natural progression is to believe in Jesus. He is the way you connect with the Father and start over as a child of God.

But things don't stop there. When you BELIEVE what Jesus says, you demonstrate it by IMMERSION in the Spirit of God.

There is no other alternative-- **to be Jesus' disciple is to do the things Jesus does with the tools that Jesus uses.**

Go ALL IN. Don't settle for humility and repentance; move on to revelation, power, love, faith, and the anointing.

Let Jesus baptize you in the Holy Spirit and FIRE.

DAY 261: Acts 23 - 26

Waiting For A Sign?

I saw a light from heaven, brighter than the sun, shining around me and those who journeyed with me.

What are you called to do? "I'm not called to do anything. I've never been knocked off my horse by a light from heaven!" **Really?**

Do you know how many people saw a light brighter than the sun and heard an audible voice to get them to pursue God's purpose for their life? **One.**

But every believer is a son or daughter-- we are ALL kings and priests to our God. We each have a unique identity and purpose that helps build the kingdom. There is no such thing as "secular" work or "just paying the bills" if you're a disciple of Jesus. **If you're waiting for a light from heaven to force you to turn around, then you are headed the wrong way!**

The usual way you find out what you're called to do is much more subtle. Sure, you'll have some encounters with God along the way, but you don't need to wait for them-- **go after them!**

Everyone starts in the same place. You humble yourself and repent, trusting Jesus to save you. Then you find someone you know is called by God, follow them, and immerse yourself in the things of the kingdom.

Paying attention to every dream, desire, impression, prophecy, and testimony, you follow the voice of God refusing to let fear hold you back. **Always assume that God has something BIG for you to do, and be willing to SERVE your way to the top.**

Treasure each encounter you have with the Lord, subtle or loud, and take action to fulfill God's call on your life.

DAY 262: Acts 27 - Romans 2

Glory, Honor, & Immortality

Eternal life to those who by patient continuance in doing good seek for glory, honor, and immortality.

Change the WAY YOU THINK! If you keep trying to improve your life as an orphan does-- posturing yourself as a victim and manipulating others for selfish and short-term gain-- you will lose in the end.

But if you SUBMIT to God, BELIEVE in Jesus, and start TALKING and ACTING as a son or daughter, then you'll win. What does that mean? How do I talk and act like a child of God?

You seek glory, honor, and immortality.

Believers long for GLORY. You should desire to walk in the same level of peace, love, joy, anointing, power, hope, faith, and influence that Jesus did.

To follow Jesus is to want HONOR. You should long to be known in heaven and hell, to walk with authority, to be famous for empowering others, and to leave a legacy for your grandchildren.

Disciples hope for IMMORTALITY. You must hunger to LIVE FOREVER in the presence of God, making an eternal impact and receiving the reward for your labor.

Not only should you want those things, but **you should SEEK them every day**, patiently adding value to more and more people. Glory, honor, and immortality make the game of life meaningful and exciting.

Whoever adds the most value to the most people using the tools Jesus provides wins!

DAY 263: Romans 3 - 6

I Reckon

Likewise you also, reckon yourselves to be dead indeed to sin, but alive to God in Christ Jesus our Lord.

It doesn't matter that Jesus died.

It makes no difference that He conquered sin and death, rising from the grave on the third day.

It's worthless that Jesus ascended into heaven and poured out the Holy Spirit, connecting heaven and earth.

All of the freedom, acceptance, power, love, and revelation that He procured does you no good.

UNLESS...

You change the way you think about yourself.

You see, Jesus did all the heavy lifting, setting the legal precedent for your freedom, and providing the grace for you to be awesome.

But unless you change the way you think about yourself, you won't benefit at all.

Paul said to **RECKON yourself dead to sin and alive to God.** That means you must **BELIEVE what Jesus did already worked, CONSIDER yourself a new person, and live as if you're amazing.**

Jim Rhon said it best in one of my favorite quotes, **"If I will change, everything will change for me."**

DAY 264: Romans 7 - 10

The Things Of The Spirit

For those who live according to the flesh set their minds on the things of the flesh, but those who live according to the Spirit, the things of the Spirit.

Paul said to set your mind on the things of the Spirit, not the things of the flesh. **What do you think he meant?** Every human being is designed by God to need certain things. We all require clean water and nutritious food, exercise, adequate sleep, clothing and shelter, love and affection, a sense of belonging, meaningful work, sexual fulfillment, and stories that fascinate us. None of those things are inherently evil-- God is the One who made us to need those things.

You cannot repent for wanting to satisfy those cravings, and they will never go away. However, it is the way we get those things that make all the difference in the world.

You see, there are only two ways to approach life-- **you are either a son or an orphan.** It was paramount that the SON OF GOD came to reconnect us with the FATHER because only a SON can make us sons. No other religion or way of thinking can reconcile our alienation from the Father.

As long as you feel like an orphan, you will set your mind on survival. You will try to fulfill your basic human needs the best you know how. **But when you are a son or daughter, you let the Father take responsibility for your needs, and you set your mind on the things of the Spirit.** You spend your time thinking about what the Spirit is saying and doing, glorifying Jesus, and adding value to people.

Jesus said to stop wasting your creativity on food and clothes and seek first the Kingdom of God, and as a result, the Father would take care of your needs.

DAY 265: Romans 11 - 14

The Renewed Mind

And do not be conformed to this world, but be transformed by the renewing of your mind, that you may prove what is that good and acceptable and perfect will of God.

What determines your ability to impact the people around you?

Is it fate? Are you waiting on God's timing? Perhaps it is your gift mix? Maybe it is the environment or the people that surround you? Could it be talent, resources, or divine favor?

I don't think so.

Jesus demonstrated and taught the perfect will of God: people reconnecting with the Father, feeling a sense of belonging, getting healthy and free, and becoming powerful builders of the Kingdom of God on the earth.

So what determines if you can prove the will of God as Jesus did?

The way you think.

Is the world supposed to get better or worse? Is God a loving Father or a cruel taskmaster? Are you supposed to touch thousands of lives or just survive to the end? Do you divide your life between secular and sacred, or are you always building the kingdom? Do your words carry authority?

Are you willing to sell, lead, go on camera, and deliver results for others, or are you just paying bills and entertaining yourself?

THE WAY YOU THINK ABOUT YOURSELF IS THE DETERMINING FACTOR WHETHER YOU IMPACT THE WORLD OR STRUGGLE TO SURVIVE.

DAY 266: Romans 15 - 1 Corinthians 2

Abundant Hope

Now may the God of hope fill you with all joy and peace in believing, that you may abound in hope by the power of the Holy Spirit.

Do you know where joy and peace come from? BELIEVING.

When your mind, emotions, speech, and actions are all aligned in pursuit of something you believe is God's will, it creates rest and happiness inside.

You FEEL great when you want the same things for yourself as God does, and HOPE abounds in your heart.

However, we usually do the opposite. We don't want to get our expectations too high because we're afraid of disappointment.

The way we talk, feel, act, and think doesn't agree with God's desires for us, and we're scared to go after stuff because we're afraid to fail.

Therefore, we live without believing, and we miss out on peace, joy, and hope.

For some reason, we think that God is going to wave His magic wand and drop something awesome in our lap, and then we'll be happy.

But it doesn't work that way. **It's the BELIEVING that makes you happy, not the fulfillment.**

It's the passionate pursuit of the dreams God put in your heart that make life worth living, not sitting on "someday" beach waiting for the perfect guy/girl/job/home/trip/opportunity to drop in your lap.

DAY 267: 1 Corinthians 3 - 6

All Things Are Yours

For all things are yours: whether Paul or Apollos or Cephas, or the world or life or death, or things present or things to come--all are yours.

Do you realize your level of ACCESS?

You didn't sign up for a cult when you began following Jesus, nor did you join a religious organization. This is not a self-help group or a ten-step program to cope with your problems. You are not jumping on the bandwagon of the latest guru to improve your life by two percent.

When you follow Jesus, you become a son or daughter of THE CREATOR. **His Spirit came to live in you, giving you ACCESS to EVERYTHING.** You have the login and password to the mind of God, and the manual to teach you how to search.

All things are yours.

Others can't understand what is going on in you because they still think like orphans.

Faith, hope, love, gratitude, forgiveness, worship, and community are not random suggestions to improve your life-- **they are the ACCESS portals** through which you receive the revelation and power to change the world.

Changing the way you think, feel, talk, and act are not religious duties earning you points so you can be rewarded in the sweet by and by.

You are the light of the world, the hope of the nations. Identifying yourself as a child of God and aligning your mind, emotions, actions, and words with His desires for you is the way the world looks like heaven.

DAY 268: 1 Corinthians 7 - 10

Run To Win

Do you not know that those who run in a race all run, but one receives the prize? Run in such a way that you may obtain it.

Run to win. It sounds simple, but it's hard to do sometimes.

Think about the areas of your life: family, friends, work, ministry, health, money. **Are you pursuing excellence in each area?**

Are you living in such a way that you become the best in the world at what you do? Why not?

There are plenty of reasons not to-- fear of failure, insecurity, emotional trauma, and stress from an overcrowded life come to mind.

But really, why not?

You don't think of yourself as a winner.

You believed the lie that your thoughts, feelings, actions, skills, speech, habits, and relationships are outside of your control.

In short, **you feel like a victim in some area of your life**. You don't think you can win, or you believe it wouldn't make a difference if you did.

BUT IT'S NOT TRUE!

Every aspect of your inner life is under your control, and you have access to the Spirit of the Living God.

RUN TO WIN.

DAY 269: 1 Corinthians 11 - 14

What Is Jesus Doing?

Imitate me, just as I also imitate Christ.

What would Jesus do? That question became popular several years ago as a way to settle a moral dilemma. If faced with two options, ask, "What would Jesus do?" and then make your decision based on what you think He would do if He were in your situation.

It's not a terrible way to make choices, I guess, but it's not what Paul taught the Corinthians. He said, "Imitate me, just as I also imitate Christ." Paul was not making moral decisions based on Jesus' track record-- **he was in a relationship with the living Christ.**

He was not asking, "What would Jesus do?" **He talked to Jesus, who was alive and well, and asked Him, "What are you doing?"** Paul knew that he was Jesus' hands and mouth on the earth, and he wanted to live in perfect alignment with what Jesus was currently doing.

There are only two options for the believer. Either you are a world changer receiving orders from heaven, or you are following a world changer and learning from them. (You can be both, by the way.) There are no survivors or spectators in the kingdom-- **there are only world changers and interns.**

If you don't fit into one of those categories, or you feel like a victim in some area of your life, CHANGE THE WAY YOU THINK.

Find a world changer and start modeling what they do. Adjust your environment-- change who you listen to, what you read and watch, where you go, who you hang out with, etc.-- and your feelings will change along with it.

DAY 270: 1 Corinthians 15 - 2 Corinthians 2

What Are Your Assumptions?

For I delivered to you first of all that which I also received: that Christ died for our sins according to the Scriptures.

The way you see the world, yourself, and God is the most important thing in life. Your perspective touches everything, influencing how you think, feel, and act, and ultimately, the results you get. **If you start with the wrong assumptions, you will end up in the wrong place.**

Here are seven key assumptions that every believer must embrace if they want to follow Jesus and impact the world:

THE WORLD IS SUPPOSED TO GET BETTER, NOT WORSE. If you believe that it's all going to fall apart in the end, you can't do the work necessary to make the world a better place.
THERE IS NO SUCH THING AS SACRED AND SECULAR. Everything we do should honor God and add value to people, including our work, rest, and entertainment.
YOUR HEART IS GOOD. What Jesus did for you worked; all that's left is to believe it.
YOU ARE NOT A VICTIM. I don't care what you went through, Jesus didn't get up from the grave so you could feel sorry for yourself.
YOU ARE NOT WAITING ON GOD. There is waiting in life, between sowing and reaping, but God already did everything necessary for you to prosper, and He is releasing life-changing ideas every day.
YOU ARE A WORLD CHANGER. There are no survivors or spectators in the Kingdom, only world changers and interns.
YOU ARE JUST ONE IDEA AWAY. If you believe the other six assumptions, and you cultivate your heart into fertile soil, **all it takes is one idea from God to turn any area of your life into a fruitful field.**

DAY 271: 2 Corinthians 3 - 6

Self-Imposed Restrictions

You are not restricted by us, but you are restricted by your own affections.

Be honest with yourself-- there is no one holding you back. It's not your parents, pastor, boss, ex-husband, or group of friends-- **you just don't want to.** You could lose the weight, write the book, make some extra money, deepen that relationship, or whatever, but the desire to do so is not as strong as the pain associated with the changes you would need to make. **So you settle into survival mode, wishing for better results without changing your behavior.** So here's the all-important QUESTION-- if desire is the ONLY way to be successful, **how do I make myself want something?** Now that's a good question, and I have an answer for you.

First, change your IDENTITY. Change the way you think about yourself by dwelling on God's purpose for your life as seen in the Bible, your prophetic words, testimonies of how God has used you, and desires He put in your heart. TALK YOURSELF INTO BECOMING WHO GOD CREATED YOU TO BE.

Next, consider the PEOPLE who would benefit from the changes you need to make. Consciously think about all of the people you care about (including yourself), and how their life would improve if you changed. LOVE IS THE BEST MOTIVATOR BY FAR, SO USE IT TO HELP YOU DO HARD THINGS.

Finally, change your ENVIRONMENT. Change what you watch, what you listen to, who you hang out with, where you go, what you read, and how you spend your time, and your feelings will begin to align with your new environment. YOU CAN CREATE DESIRE BY CHANGING THE STORIES YOU CONNECT WITH.

DAY 272: 2 Corinthians 7 - 10

Follow Through

Now you also must complete the doing of it; that as there was a readiness to desire it, so there also may be a completion out of what you have.

You said you wanted to do it. **Halfway through the how-to book you bought, something came up, and you never got back to it.** Your intentions are good. Even after all this time, the desire is still there.

BUT YOU HAVEN'T DONE IT.

Like the Corinthians, you set out a year ago to finish that project that would transform your life and add value to a bunch of people, but there it sits, gathering dust.

Are you waiting for permission? Is fear holding you back?

I understand how overwhelmed you feel when you think about all that needs doing and how little time there is to do it. Whatever the reason you haven't done it yet, it's not too late.

DO IT TODAY!

Don't wait until tomorrow. Forget your crazy schedule this week and do it right now. Make the call, pay for the service, set up the account, write the check, set up the meeting, or whatever you need to do.

Fear doesn't tell you what to do anymore.

You're not the same person as you were a year ago.

You have permission to BE AWESOME today. Just do it.

DAY 273: 2 Corinthians 11 - Galatians 1

Living Without Anxiety

Become complete. Be of good comfort, be of one mind, live in peace; and the God of love and peace will be with you.

Become complete, be single-minded, and live at peace. That's the advice Paul gave the Corinthians, and wow, could we benefit from it today. **But how?**

How do we live without anxiety? I'm not going to pretend to have all the answers, but I have found one thing that makes a big difference. COMMITMENT.

It's not difficult circumstances that cause stress-- **it's a divided heart.** It's when we're unsure of how we feel, what we think, or what to do that we get anxious.

So here's a simple trick that helps a ton-- **make a short-term commitment.** Let's say I don't know whether to go through door number one or door number two, and I keep going back and forth on the pros and cons of each. **The longer I linger in indecision, the more stressed out I get**.

The best way to live at peace is to go all-in on one of them for a limited time (a week, month, or year, etc.) You're not deciding what to do forever, you're resolving to do something until the end of the year with all your might, and then reevaluate.

The same process works for your thoughts and feelings as well. If you're not sure what you believe about something, pick a side and go deep for a while. Don't allow yourself to argue until you have spent the allotted time all-in. **It works-- try it.**

DAY 274: Galatians 2 - 5

Why Not You?

God shows personal favoritism to no man--for those who seemed to be something added nothing to me.

God shows personal favoritism to no one. Period.

That means all those people out there changing the world have no more favor than you do.

They're not special. They weren't born that way. They're just like you.

So why are they making a significant impact, and you're not? Three reasons:

They think of themselves the same way God thinks about them.

They develop emotional wholeness internally and in their relationships with others.

They leverage time and money for maximum impact.

It's not our circumstances or some magic fairy dust that distinguishes between those "favored" by God and us ordinary folks-- **it's just faith, hope, and love.**

How you think about yourself will determine your impact on the world.

So why not you? Why can't you change the world?

You can, and you should. **Nothing is standing between you and a fruitful life except you.**

DAY 275: Galatians 6 - Ephesians 3

What Do You Pray For?

That the God of our Lord Jesus Christ, the Father of glory, may give to you the spirit of wisdom and revelation in the knowledge of Him.

Have you ever studied the prayers in the Bible? It's fascinating what the Holy Spirit prompted guys like Paul to pray because it gives us insight into what we need the most.

The prayers we often hear (or pray) sound something like this, "God, heal so and so," or "Father, I need money for that thing," or "Why did this happen to me?" But that's not the kind of prayers modeled or taught in the Bible.

In Ephesians 1, Paul writes to a group of believers he has never met, letting them know what he is praying for them. **Do you know what the ONLY request he makes for them, the thing that would push the domino over leading to an abundant life?**

REVELATION.

Paul prays that they would understand WHO THEY ARE and WHAT THEY ALREADY HAVE ACCESS TO. **He knows that if the Ephesians get that, they get everything.** The same is true for you and me. **When we THINK correctly about ourselves, the entire kingdom opens up to us.** Jesus already took care of the legal stuff for us to be AWESOME, but we can only access what we BELIEVE.

When you pray, switch your focus from asking for the thing you want (which implies you have no authority) to requesting more UNDERSTANDING about who you are and the power already at work in you.

DAY 276: Ephesians 4 - Philippians 1

Walk Worthy

I, therefore, the prisoner of the Lord, beseech you to walk worthy of the calling with which you were called.

Can I be real with you? The old religious model where there is one "minister" for every hundred believers is, well, stupid. Did Jesus rise from the grave and pour out the Holy Spirit so a bunch of victims could gather to receive "ministry" every week?

Are we supposed to spend all week doing jobs we don't like, stressed out about money, destroying our health, arguing with our family, and then medicating the pain with all sorts of nonsense? Is this what Jesus had in mind, a group of unhealthy, broken victims going to the hospital (I mean church) now and then to get treatment? **I think not.**

As Paul explains in Ephesians 4, every believer has a calling. We are all kings and priests with a special grace from Jesus to build each other up and make the world a better place. **It irks me to see the light of the world, the people who are the answer to every problem on earth, hiding in a corner trying to hang on until someone comes to rescue them from this "awful" world.**

This is our planet. We are sons and daughters of God, ruling with Him to break the back of orphan thinking and bring His peace to society.

There are no orphans, victims, beggars, or survivors in the kingdom. You are either a world changer or an intern world changer; those are the only options.

We all heal the sick, hear from God, worship with abandon, and use the grace Jesus gave us to add value to others.

DAY 277: Philippians 2 - Colossians 1

Think Like Jesus

Let this mind be in you which was also in Christ Jesus.

How did Jesus think about himself?

Was He anxious, insecure, or fearful?

Of course not.

Was He prideful and arrogant, bullying His way to the front of the line?

No way.

Orphans must choose between playing the victim to manipulate people into giving them what they want and bullying others to take it, but sons and daughters don't have to play that game.

Because we are already safe, loved, secure, accepted, and provided for, we can rest.

The Father's purpose for Jesus was to make Him so famous that everyone in the world would know His name and submit to His leadership. You can't get any bigger than that.

However, the Father's plan for how Jesus would get there involved humility, service, and sacrificing His life.

Jesus said yes to both. He SUBMITTED to being great and serving His way to the top.

So how does Jesus think? **He thinks like a Son, and so should you.**

DAY 278: Colossians 2 - 1 Thessalonians 1

Set Your Mind

Set your mind on things above, not on things on the earth.

God designed you to live free and exercise authority in every area of your life. He doesn't want to control you; in fact, He refuses to.

Jesus came to reconnect you to the Father, but you don't get the benefits of what He did unless you live aware and in agreement with Him. Therefore, **what you think about is the most important thing in the world.**

When you set your mind on things like who God says you are, what Jesus did for you, what the Holy Spirit is saying and doing, and how you can partner with Him to add value to others, you create a productive ecosystem in your soul.

That awareness causes agreement, and your agreement gives you access to heaven. Instead of drawing from your own resources, you get access to God's love, grace, power, revelation, and wealth.

You were never meant to live disconnected from the Father, drifting through life on your own.

You were designed to stay connected, and it's your THOUGHT LIFE that builds the bridge.

You don't have to fill your day with office gossip, cat videos, and negative news reports. You're not required to worry about money and wallow in loneliness.

You control what you think about, so set your mind on things that set you up to succeed.

DAY 279: 1 Thessalonians 2 - 5

Growing In Love

But we urge you, brethren, that you increase more and more.

What does love look like? More specifically, **how do you show someone who doesn't feel loved that you care about them?**

I'm sure there are many ways, but I want to highlight one.

You listen to them.

You take the time to hear what is going on in their lives, how they feel, and why they feel that way.

It's not complicated, but it can be hard to do.

Often, when people are hurt or struggling, they lash out in some way.

If you can get past your initial reaction to put your guard up and hear what they are trying to say, then you're doing better than most.

But many times it's hard for them to understand or explain what they're feeling, so you have to add some patience and compassion and help them discover why they're hurt.

Be careful not to try to fix everything or give premature advice, but instead ask simple questions covered with grace.

Lead them to a place of greater awareness while making then feel safe.

Nothing communicates love like a genuine, patient ear ready to hear what is on their heart.

DAY 280: 2 Thessalonians 1 - 1 Timothy 1

Fight For Your Future

This charge I commit to you, son Timothy, according to the prophecies previously made concerning you, that by them you may wage the good warfare.

You are not an accident. You are here for a reason, and the world needs you at your best.

Many of us, however, are passive when it comes to walking out our identity and purpose. We have a vague idea of who God called us to be, but **we sit around "waiting on God" instead of pursuing our passion.**

There are three fundamental ways to know what your purpose is: **prophecies, testimonies, and desires.**

God talks to us through mental impressions, dreams, Scripture verses, unusual circumstances, songs, sermons, and prophecies from others to leave clues about who we are. Pay attention to what He says and take it seriously.

Also, watch for patterns of how God uses you to add value to others-- those testimonies are an indicator of your identity.

Finally, don't discount your desires. The longings inside you were placed there by God to drive you into your purpose.

Take the time to get clear about your future, but don't stop there. **Merely knowing why you were born doesn't make it happen, you have to FIGHT for it.**

Use the prophecies, testimonies, and desires to launch an all-out war on survival and complacency, and do whatever it takes to fulfill your role on the earth.

DAY 281: 1 Timothy 2 - 5

Go All In

Meditate on these things; give yourself entirely to them, that your progress may be evident to all.

Do you know what will change the world (and make me smile until my face hurts)?

The world will change **when you know how God thinks about you.** Pretty simple, right?

Oh, there's one more thing. **You must think about yourself the same way-- you can't disagree with Him.**

When you know how God feels about you and why you were born, and you live in full agreement with it, look out!

My dream is for you to understand your IDENTITY and pursue it with passion. Nothing else would make me, God, or you happier, or have a more significant effect on the planet.

Except for one thing-- **you making money doing what you're called to do.** Now that would be AMAZING!

Imagine it (c'mon, just let yourself imagine for a second.) **What if you were crystal clear about your identity and purpose, and you made your living doing the thing God called you to do.**

You could FOCUS on the thing that makes you smile AND add tons of value to others AND master your craft AND care for your family at the same time. **Go for it.**

DAY 282: 1 Timothy 6 - 2 Timothy 3

7 Stages Of A Fruitful Life

For God has not given us a spirit of fear, but of power and of love and of a sound mind.

There are seven stages we go through if we are to live a fruitful life.

Remember, in this analogy, **your heart is the soil, the seeds are ideas God gives you, and the fruit is the things you produce to help others.**

1. BUY IN. It's time to get rid of shame and blame, take responsibility for your heart, and believe that you are supposed to live a fruitful life. Unless you take OWNERSHIP of your thoughts, feelings, words, and actions and say no to a victim mentality, you will never get past this stage.
2. SOIL PREP. Once you're ALL-IN, it's time for personal growth. You immerse yourself in learning, doing everything you can to master your health, relationships, time, money, thought life, emotions, and confidence.
3. CONTRIBUTION. Now your heart is fertile, and you start trying to help others any way you can. You grow a little of everything, paying attention to what produces the most fruit, adds the most value, people are willing to pay for, is sustainable, and you enjoy.
4. PRODUCT CREATION. This stage is all about narrowing your focus. You find out what is working, and you do more of it. Along the way, you eliminate the things that don't produce the results you want for yourself and others and master the things that do.
5. PLATFORM BUILDING. Now that you have a way to add value, you begin expanding your distribution. You take your fruit to market and gather a group of raving fans.
6. SCALE. Once things are working, you build a team to multiply your effectiveness.
7. IMPACT. At this stage, you fine tune everything to see how you can add the most value to the most people.

DAY 283: 2 Timothy 4 - Titus 3

Preach The Word!

Preach the word! Be ready in season and out of season. Convince, rebuke, exhort, with all longsuffering and teaching.

When most people think about preaching they picture an old white guy standing behind a pulpit explaining a Bible verse to a congregation, but I want to expand your understanding of the concept.

The message of the kingdom is simple: Jesus, the Son of God, came to earth to invite all of us to **stop living like orphans.** He reconnected us with the Father, and together we make the world a better place.

Preaching is marketing, plain and simple. It's telling stories to persuade someone to stop living like an orphan or a victim, believe in Jesus, and start thinking like a son or daughter of God.

We preach to help others adopt a new IDENTITY. Once they have done that, then and only then can they learn how to do life better.

So, whether you are a singer or musician, health and fitness professional, writer and speaker, business owner, government official, or just a parent or grandparent, the job is the same-- **preach the word.**

Help others think like sons and daughters, and then after they have bought in and are listening to you, teach them how to live like one.

We are not in the business of using shame to manipulate people into following a list of rules. We aggressively market the best news in the world, **"You are not an accident. You are not alone. You are a son or daughter of the Creator, and together we add value to others and make the world look like heaven."**

DAY 284: Philemon - Hebrews 3

Becoming Effective

That the sharing of your faith may become effective by the acknowledgment of every good thing which is in you in Christ Jesus.

There are four kinds of people in the world.

First, there are the quitters. They are in such pain that they can't see a reason to go on. **Next, there are the survivors.** These guys are hanging on, working hard, trying to keep up with their bills and maintain their relationships. **Third, there are the achievers.** They figure out some of the principles of life and use them to their advantage, but they lack purpose. **Finally, there are the world changers.** This group know their God-given identity and purpose and have mastered the skills to distribute what they offer to others effectively.

In the book of Philemon (which is an unbelievable sales letter by the way), Paul reveals the key to becoming effective. He says that if you want to share what you have with the world, **you must first acknowledge what God put inside you.** God dreamed about you in your mother's womb and fashioned you with a specific purpose. Shame, insecurity, blame, fear, anger, depression, and anxiety try to steal your identity away, but YOU DON'T HAVE TO LET THAT HAPPEN.

If you're struggling, try this exercise. Write down **something God said about you** (prophetic word, dream, scripture, etc.), **some way He used you before** to help others, and **a big desire** you have.

Now combine them in your mind to form a snapshot of the purpose God has for you. **Imagine yourself as the BEST IN THE WORLD at adding value to those people in that way, and then start living AS IF IT'S ALREADY TRUE.**

DAY 285: Hebrews 4 - 7

Don't Get Sluggish

That you do not become sluggish, but imitate those who through faith and patience inherit the promises.

Have you ever heard the saying that the hardest part of doing anything is getting started? **The person who said that probably never finished anything, because that's nonsense.**

The most challenging part of doing anything worth doing is **right smack in the middle.**

When you start, you're excited. Ideas flow and motivation surges at the beginning, but as time passes and the work gets tough, things begin to fall apart. Distractions and excuses fill up the empty part of your brain that used to contain all of those fantastic ideas you had at first.

Towards the end of a project, when you can see the finished line, suddenly motivation returns and pushes you onward. You look around, wondering where it came from and where it was from mile two until twenty-five of the marathon.

The first mile is exciting, and number twenty-six is rewarding, but **those twenty-four lonely miles in the middle are where you win the race.** If you're in the thick of it and are beginning to get sluggish, I feel you.

Don't quit. Split your goal up into manageable chunks and celebrate every mile marker you pass.

Remember who you are, the way you will feel when you cross the finished line, and the people who are counting on you, and KEEP MAKING PROGRESS.

DAY 286: Hebrews 8 - 11

The Conscience

Let us draw near with a true heart in full assurance of faith, having our hearts sprinkled from an evil conscience and our bodies washed with pure water.

God designed you to be awesome.

The way your mind and heart interact with your body, others, and the spirit realm is incredible. Have you ever stopped to think about it?

Following Jesus has nothing to with religion. An external set of rules to regulate behavior may be necessary for society, but that's not why Jesus came.

He came so you can THINK and FEEL like a son or daughter.

Before Christ, there was no way for your conscience to be clear; **you always felt like there was something wrong.**

Jesus made it possible for you to FEEL safe, confident, happy, secure, and clean. Through Him, you can walk down the street with full control of your mind and no sense of shame or guilt.

Believing in Jesus enables you to be like Him, fully integrating the natural and the supernatural. You can now look at anyone and genuinely want the best for them. You can hear from God, make demons leave, heal diseases, and forgive sins. Your body, work, creative expressions, and relationships are all GOOD.

If you live with guilt, shame, fear, or bitterness you have believed a lie. Draw near to God with confidence and meditate on the truth of the gospel. You too can experience life with a clear conscience.

DAY 287: Hebrews 12 - James 2

Doing The Word

But be doers of the word, and not hearers only, deceiving yourselves.

God has a purpose for your life, and **most likely, you already know what it is.** You may not be clear about all the details, but you got a general idea.

The Father drops hints in our dreams, stirs up our desires, prophesies through our friends, reveals secrets to our mentors, and uses our past testimonies to predict our future.

All creation is begging for you to understand who you are and start living it out.

The question is not whether you've heard from God.

The question is WHAT ARE YOU DOING ABOUT IT?

James tells it to us straight-- if you want God's blessing, you must grow the ideas He gives you.

"Where do I start?" you say. It depends on where you're at right now.

Your life is like a garden. First, you prepare your heart by developing confidence, becoming emotionally whole, and learning to focus.

Then, you practice hearing from God, turning His ideas into desires, writing them down in detail, and planting them in your mind and letting them grow.

Finally, you align your life with those desires by weeding out other things and watering what you want to bear fruit.

DAY 288: James 3 - 1 Peter 1

Changing Course

Look also at ships: although they are so large and are driven by fierce winds, they are turned by a very small rudder wherever the pilot desires.

So, you want to change your life.

You're tired of merely surviving-- you want to do something that matters.

Enough of avoiding mirrors because you're disgusted by what you see, working a dead-end job that you can't stand, scrapping every month for barely enough to take care of your family, or feeling sorry for yourself one minute and then beating yourself up the next.

You want to be proud of yourself, to honor God with the gifts He gave you, and add real value to those around you.

You know it's going to take hard work and patience-- you're ready for that.

But where do you start?

How do you change the course of your life?

Just like a giant cruise ship changes direction with a tiny rudder, **you steer your life with your tongue.**

The way you talk to yourself, about yourself, and to others determines the direction you go.

So, you want to change your life? **Change the way you talk.**

DAY 289: 1 Peter 2 - 5

Never Stop Growing

As newborn babes, desire the pure milk of the word, that you may grow thereby.

Did you know that the average person who listens to podcasts during the day makes three times as much as someone who listens to music? Interesting, isn't it? **Those who are hungry to learn out-produce those who are just passing the time three to one.**

Why do you think that is? Obviously, those eager to learn will end up more knowledgeable than the others, but I think there's more to it than that.

I believe it has to do with identity (the way we think about ourselves.)

If you're a farmer producing crops to feed your community and provide for your family, then every detail matters. You need understanding about soil, weather, timing, markets, seeds, leadership, hiring, sales, and equipment.

But if you are a laborer picking tomatoes in a field getting paid by the hour, then all you care about is passing the time and trying to have fun while you work.

A simple mindset shift from survivor to producer creates the hunger to learn and triples your fruitfulness.

Of course, the principle doesn't just apply to money. In every area of your life-- business, relationships, health, ministry, community-- **start thinking of yourself as a producer.**

Stay hungry to learn, feeding on what God says about you and how you can add more value to others, and expect your results to grow along with your mind and heart.

DAY 290: 2 Peter 1 - 1 John 1

Layers Of A Fruitful Life

For if these things are yours and abound, you will be neither barren nor unfruitful in the knowledge of our Lord Jesus Christ.

Fruitfulness is the ability to produce something that adds significant value to others. It is the process of receiving an idea from God, growing it, and distributing it in a way that impacts the world. Jesus said that the way we glorify the Father, the entire point of the Christian life, is to **bear much fruit.**

So here's the question. **Why is it that one person can hear an idea and grow it into something that changes people's lives, while someone else gets the same idea and nothing happens?**

Those who remain unfruitful don't understand the process. We want to go straight from faith (our belief and confidence in God) to love (adding significant value to others), but we skip the steps in between.

Peter reminds us that believing in God is not enough to make you fruitful; there are layers in every fertile heart.

You start with **faith** (the way you think about God), but then you add **identity** (thinking of yourself the same way God thinks of you.) After identity, you add **knowledge** (the ideas you hear in your interaction with God.) From there you must develop **self-control** (the ability to motivate yourself.) Then you add **perseverance**, and after that, **integrity.** Next, you add **kindness** (your interpersonal communication skills), and then finally you get to **love.**

DAY 291: 1 John 2 - 5

Play To Win

For this purpose the Son of God was manifested, that He might destroy the works of the devil.

JOHN: I know this is a loaded question, but why did you come to the earth?

JESUS: Well, **I didn't come here to lose.** My Father sent Me to do a job, and I fulfilled His mandate perfectly.

JOHN: And what mandate was that?

JESUS: **To destroy the works of the devil.**

JOHN: Wow, that sounds aggressive. I thought you're the champion of meekness and humility?

JESUS: I am the KING of agreeing with My Father, changing the course of history, instituting the kingdom of God, restoring humanity, and leaving no doubt about who is in charge.

JOHN: I don't think I've ever seen this side of you. Are you always like this?

JESUS: I am full of compassion for those the devil has lied to, and I intend to lead them back to the Father. But **I don't play for second place. The Father sent me to change the world, so that's what I'm doing.**

JOHN: This may be inappropriate, but **why do so many of your followers seem so, well, weak?**

JESUS: The enemy has tricked them into believing that they're still orphans, spreading lies to convince them to survive instead of thriving, but that's changing. **This generation is the greatest generation to ever live.**

JOHN: How so?

JESUS: **More people than ever before know that their voice matters, and together we are beating disease, loneliness, addiction, poverty, racism, and the victim mentality.**

JOHN: Thank you so much for your time. Any final thoughts?

JESUS: **PLAY TO WIN. Destroy the works of the devil in your own life, and then attack the problems I called you to solve.** We got this.

DAY 292: 2 John 1 - Revelation 1

Prosper In All Things

Beloved, I pray that you may prosper in all things and be in health, just as your soul prospers.

God designed you to prosper in every area of your life. Your relationships, money, work, health, ministry, and hobbies should all be fruitful, adding value to your life and others.

Then why don't we prosper? **What is holding us back?** We think that our prosperity relates to a decision God makes, so we continue to plug along waiting on God to favor us. We associate prosperity with faithfulness, like if we keep showing up, eventually God will notice-- but that's not the way it works.

Athletes don't become the best in the world at their sport merely because they show up for practice every day, and workers don't become wealthy because they're always on time.

The fruitfulness of our health, wealth, and relationships correlates directly to the prosperity of our souls. Our THOUGHTS, FEELINGS, and DESIRES must flourish before our life can. We must think about ourselves the same way God does, learn to overcome negative emotions, motivate ourselves, persevere, seek out the best coaches, and follow through internally before it shows on the outside.

You're not waiting on God, you're not going to win the lottery, faithfulness is not enough to produce fruit.

Align yourself with God's purpose, face your fears, believe the truth, do hard things, solve problems, and learn new skills. **The world inside you will eventually manifest in every area of your life.**

DAY 293: Revelation 2 - 5

Your New Name

I will give him a white stone, and on the stone a new name written which no one knows except him who receives it.

Your parents tried (well, most of them did.) They attempted to protect and raise you the best they knew how, but when you were born, they were still immature themselves.

Some of them abandoned, abused, or neglected you, leaving deep wounds. Others worked hard to give you what they never had growing up, setting you up to succeed.

But if we're honest (I'm speaking as a parent myself), **most of the time parents are just winging it**, doing the best they can with what they have.

The environment we grew up in and the names our parents gave us formed our identities, and they didn't always get it right.

But there's good news-- Jesus is offering you a new name based on the Father's original purpose for your life.

The Father dreamed about you before you were born, contemplating the incredible impact you would have on the planet. Then life happened, piling heaps of garbage on your true identity and leaving you insecure and unaware of the Father's plan.

Listen as Jesus speaks to your heart right now, **"If you overcome, I'll tell you who you really are. It will be our secret; no one else needs to know. I know your heart-- I see you without the pile of garbage covering your identity and purpose. Allow Me the privilege of revealing it to you."**

DAY 294: Revelation 6 - 9

No Regrets

The Lamb who is in the midst of the throne will shepherd them and lead them to living fountains of waters. And God will wipe away every tear from their eyes.

Life hurts sometimes.

Accidents surprise us, slander irritates us, and betrayal smacks us in the face. Death, disease, and divorce gang up to push us into a ditch, and they'll keep us there if we let them.

But there is an answer, a way to experience real healing and happiness in this life and the next, and His name is Jesus.

He is the only way to go from feeling like an orphan to living as a son or daughter of the Creator, and He is the only way to emotional wholeness.

If you believe in Jesus and follow Him into eternal life, one day many years from now, you will be resting in His love, free from all pain.

You are safe, forever.

There's only one thing you can't undo, a pain that will last longer than you intend and hurt more than any other-- regret.

DON'T LIVE WITH REGRET!

Do what you're called to do with all your might, take risks, and love people well. Forgive yourself for the mistakes you made and make the changes you need to make.

THIS IS YOUR OPPORTUNITY, SEIZE IT!

DAY 295: Revelation 10 - 13

He Shall Reign

The kingdoms of this world have become the kingdoms of our Lord and of His Christ, and He shall reign forever and ever!

Have you ever wondered, "who's in charge around here?" **Well, you are.**

Adam and Eve gave their dominion of the earth to the enemy when they voluntarily listened to and obeyed him. The result was a series of massive empires ruled by power-hungry dictators trying to take over the world. Satan ruled the world through fear, intimidation, greed, lust, hatred, and deception.

But Jesus put an end to his schemes, conquering death and taking back the leadership of the planet. Do you know what Jesus did with the authority He gained? **He gave it back to you.**

Since then, we the people have decided the fate of every generation.

Don't get me wrong, Jesus is still in charge-- but He doesn't rule like the enemy. **Control and manipulation are not His style.**

He empowers people and gives them the ideas, tools, and favor they need to succeed.

His political agenda includes every person on the planet voluntarily connecting with the Father, making their own decisions, and living happy, healthy, and productive lives.

The only thing the world needs to get better is for you to think about yourself the way God does, spend time with Jesus soaking up His ideas, and then solve the problems He puts on your heart.

DAY 296: Revelation 14 - 17

The Next Jesus Movement

Then I looked, and behold, a Lamb standing on Mount Zion, and with Him one hundred and forty-four thousand.

Can I prophecy to you for a minute? I want to tell you about the next Jesus movement and the emerging generation of revivalists because I think you might be one of them.

God is calling a new breed of world changers. Their core values are the same as every generation of believers-- they believe the Bible, are loyal to Jesus, love worship and community, and practice the essential elements of the faith. **But the expression of their faith is radically different.** They are a band of CREATIVE ENTREPRENEURS who believe the world is supposed to get better, not worse, and they are ALL IN to help solve the problems facing their generation.

This group couldn't care less about denominations, and they include women and men from every race, age, and nationality. **Each of them MAKE MONEY doing what they're called to do, allowing them to FOCUS on mastering their craft.** They are artists, speakers, authors, tech specialists, singers, musicians, and coaches with a message to share and a tribe to gather.

This crowd doesn't reserve spiritual gifts for church services, **they hear from God about business and relationships every day,** and they cooperate with the Holy Spirit at all times. They are confident in their IDENTITIES, emotionally whole, and AMBITIOUS. Not one of them is hiding in a corner waiting to be rescued, **choosing instead to develop themselves into the kind of person who makes an IMPACT.**

What do you think? Do you want to be a part of the next Jesus movement?

DAY 297: Revelation 18 - 22

He Who Overcomes

He who overcomes shall inherit all things, and I will be his God and he shall be My son.

Do you know what I want for you? **I want you to feel like a son or daughter of God.**

I want you to never worry about money again and experience the safety of being a part of a family. **I want you to be happy.**

I want you to find your identity and purpose, and walk it out with joy.

I want you to do meaningful work that adds value to people and makes the world a better place.

I want you to live off your inheritance from your Father, and feel the bliss of God's presence.

I want you to hear from heaven and understand what to do with the ideas God gives you. **I want you to be proud of yourself.**

I want you to know the joy of treating others according to their possibilities, not their problems.

I want you to feel beautiful, appreciated, and loved.

I want you to relax, have fun, and enjoy your life.

You can experience all those things and more, but you must OVERCOME your insecurity, fear, doubt, pain, anger, opposition, and apathy.

Think about yourself the way God does, and let's change the world together.

DAY 298

Five Years From Now

Five years from now, what will be the fruit of your life?

Based on the last few thousand years of recorded history, I can promise you a few things.

The government of your nation will be about the same as it is now.

Some of your friends will continue to encourage you, and some will keep whining and complaining.

Your family will be about like it is right now.

The laws, taxes, and economy will not be noticeably different.

Fall will come after summer, winter after fall, and then spring will follow winter.

God will be the same, as will the Bible.

You will continue to have good ideas, opportunities, and encounters with God. You will also experience difficulties and setbacks.

Everything will be almost exactly as it is now, **except you.**

For your life to change, you have to change. You must think better, feel happier, and want more.

Your fruitfulness does not depend on God, others, or your environment--it's up to you.

DAY 299

Identity & Intimacy

If you haven't noticed by now, **I want you to live a fruitful life.** (And God does too!)

I want you to move **out of survival** (going around and around in the wilderness paying bills and putting out fires), **into a life of impact.**

Your life should produce more than what you need to exist-- **there should be something specific that you grow an abundance of that adds significant value to others.**

It may be a physical product, service, experience, message, or community, and it should draw people closer to the Father and improve their health, standard of living, or relationships.

There are only two variables that can increase your fruitfulness-- **identity and intimacy.**

You must either think about yourself better or spend more time with Jesus hearing what He has to say, or both.

Now you know what to focus on.

Develop your confidence, happiness, and focus, and then listen to Jesus more.

If you do those two things, you will live a fruitful life.

DAY 300

Become A Professional

I want to challenge you one more time-- **find out why you're on the planet.**

Go back through all of your prophetic words, Scripture verses that stood out to you, dreams, and encounters with God.

Layer on top of that all the times God used you to help others in a significant way. Those are your testimonies, and if you have tried to love others long enough, **they reveal a pattern about who you are.**

Add to your prophecies and testimonies your big dreams and desires and you have a pretty good picture of why you're here.

Now that you know your identity (at least you're starting to), **find a way to make money fulfilling your purpose.**

Don't just go through the motions!

Find a job that allows you to add value to others, pursue a leadership role that lets you develop people, start your own business, or use your talents to help someone else succeed.

When you make a living in the crossroads where your identity, purpose, desires, and talents meet, and you find the people and the products that allow you to add the most value, good things happen.

You begin to focus on what you do best, become proficient at it, and enjoy the process, which in turn makes the world a much better place.

Tired of living in survival mode?

Connect with me on Facebook, Instagram, and the web **@johnbradbury.co** to get the accountability, inspiration, coaching, and community you need to live a fruitful life and make a living making an impact.

22786535R00187

Made in the USA
Lexington, KY
14 December 2018